THE ESSENCE OF WISDOM

Parables from the Prophet and His Companions

THE ESSENCE
OF WISDOM

Parables from the Prophet
and His Companions

Kemal Turan

New Jersey

Published by Tughra Books
335 Clifton Ave., Clifton, NJ, 07011, USA

www.tughrabooks.com

Library of Congress Cataloging-in-Publication Data Available

ISBN: 978-1-59784-263-1

Translated by Zaineb Mahmout
Edited by Jeniffer Knight-Arı

TABLE OF CONTENTS

INTRODUCTION

One of the two powerful foundations of Islam, the Sunnah, or the practices of the Prophet, were meticulously recorded, memorized, and reached the present without being changed or amended. The Sunnah is the Prophet's way of life, the way of living Islam, the example of morality conveyed by God. The Prophet was a conveyer of divine wisdom. Throughout history, many have spoken words of excellence and wisdom in accordance to their ability; however, the Prophet's words bore a unique depth of perspective, one that is unequaled in pleasure and distinctly delightful to hear. The Prophet's words are a source of wisdom from beyond; his every word moved hearts and astonished minds.

This book is a collection of parables (representations and metaphors) based on the words of the Prophet. On occasion, the Prophet would portray a truth by telling a story. Various topics are covered in these narratives of the Prophet. As it was impossible to relate all these subjects in a book, this work is rather a compilation of stories selected according to their length in the hadiths (traditions of the Prophet), and the lessons and objectives to be learned. The book approaches the stories in a different style; certain additions, not found in the original text of the hadith, were made in order to piece the story together in its entirety. Names have been given to certain characters referred to as "a person" in the original texts. However, while making these additions, care has been taken to reveal the stories, and their meaning, in the true spirit of Islamic perception.

These stories were written in an easy-to-read style, comprehensible to people of all levels of understanding, along with an explanation of the warnings and lessons to be derived. In the introduction, and in each story's conclusion, additional information was included to present these stories in a complete, comprehensive manner, in order for the moral to be crystallized in the mind of the reader.

Although the examples related in this book are based on the Prophet's words, the words in the stories are not identical to the words used by the Prophet. However, the messages conveyed by the book are faithful to the messages of the hadiths. Because the wording here is not identical to the hadith sources, the sources are specified not in footnotes, but in the reference list at the end of the book. It is our duty to make every effort possible to convey the words of faith. However, manifesting faith into the human heart is, without doubt, only by the will of God.

THREE PEOPLE IN A CAVE

Three men set out on a journey together. After walking for hours, they were exhausted. The sun had almost set, when the sky opened up and began to pour rain. One of the men said:

"We have done enough walking for today. It is almost dark, and it has started to rain. We can continue the journey early in the morning. There is a cave up in this mountain, we can eat and shelter there for the night."

With great difficulty, the three eventually reached the cave. Their clothes were soaked, and without wasting any time, they built a fire. As they warmed up and dried their clothes by the heat of the fire, a horrific sound terrified the three men. At first they thought it was an earthquake.

Due to the heavy rain, an enormous rock had tumbled down from the mountain and blocked the cave entrance. The three men rushed over, but the rock nearly covered the entire opening. It was very dark outside, and the three men were afraid. But they were also very tired from their journey, so they decided to sleep and try to find a way out of the cave in the morning.

Morning came, and thin rays of sunlight pierced tiny gaps in the barrier. The three men pushed the rock with all their strength, but in vain, for the rock did not budge. They tried again and again, but there still was no movement.

The men began to worry. If they called out, nobody could hear them; it was deserted and there was a slim chance of passerby. They had enough water and food for only two days. All means of escape faded into impossibility.

Then one of the men had an idea:

"Turning to God Almighty is our only chance. If each of us presents a deed that we believe to be approved of by God, and then by virtue of that deed, we pray for the rock to move, He may take pity on us."

The men agreed, knowing their only hope was to turn to the Almighty Creator, Who creates all means and solutions.

The first among them said:

"My mother and father were very old. I never allowed even my children to eat before my parents had eaten. One day I went out to gather some wood. It took longer than I expected so I returned home later than usual. As soon as I came home, I milked the goats and took the milk to my parents. But because it was late, they were sleeping. They were sleeping so peacefully that I did not have the heart to wake them, so I sat with the bowl of milk in my hand and waited. I sat there until early the next morning. Eventually they woke up, and I gave them the milk to drink. O Lord, I performed this deed to earn Your pleasure. I plead with You, O Lord — move this rock by virtue of my deed."

The men stared at the rock, and noticed a slight movement. They were excited and rushed over to the cave entrance. The rock had moved a little, but it was still impossible to escape.

Then the second man spoke:

"My uncle has a daughter, I was very fond of her and I wanted to be in a more intimate relationship with her. But every time I approached her, she rejected me. A short time later, there was a drought in the region. My uncle was already quite poor, and with the shortage of supplies became even poorer. She was forced to come to me for help. I was quite wealthy at the time. This was a great opportunity, so I told her that I would help if she submitted herself to me, and that I would not help if she refused. The poor girl had no choice but to accept my proposal or she and her family would perish. When I was alone with her at last, she said: 'Fear God! You know very well what you are doing is wrong, and that it is our duty to abstain from whatever God forbids.' I was persuaded by her words, and although I had the power to fulfill my desires, I changed my mind. I gave her money and sent her home, and I told my cousin that I did not expect her to return any of the money. O Lord! I performed this deed solely to gain Your pleasure. I am begging and pleading with You to save us from this cave by virtue of my deed."

Suddenly the rock moved again, but there still was not enough of a gap to escape.

Then the third man explained:

"Some men worked for me for awhile, and I paid each of them as soon as the work was finished, except for one man who did not collect his wages. Assuming that he would return in the near future, I purchased a cow with the money. Several years passed, and that cow gave birth to many calves. With the profits from these animals, one single cow had turned into a large herd of animals. Years later, the man returned and asked for the wages I owed him. Pointing to the huge herd, I told the man that all of the animals belonged to him. He was shocked, and said: 'Please do not tease me. I know it has been a long time, but I just want the wages that you owe me.' I replied: 'No, you have misunderstood. I am not teasing. I purchased one cow with the money I owed you. Over the years, the number of animals increased, and eventually became an entire herd. It is all yours. Take them with my blessing.' So the man gathered all the animals, thanked me and left. O Lord, I did this solely with the intention of earning Your pleasure. I plead with You to save us by virtue of this deed."

After this supplication, the huge rock moved once again, and left an opening large enough to pass through. Delighted, the three men prostrated in gratitude.

Reflections

Our mothers and fathers are entrusted to us by God. Respecting our parents is an obligation, but we should realize that pleasing our parents also pleases God.

When the conditions are ideal for sin, abstaining from sin because of the fear of God brings one closer to his Creator. He is adored by God, and by His servants.

An employer should give his employees their due, and never oppress them. In a hadith, the Prophet of God said: "Do not withhold the rights of others"[1] and "do not demand what is not your right." An employee must fulfill his duties, and should be given his salary before his sweat has dried. An employer must consider his employee as a brother or sister, and ensure that they benefit from the profits of the workplace.

Both the owner and the laborer must be aware that they are watched by God. Both the employer's capital and the employee's labor will then be considered mutually valuable, and disputes about exploitation or conflicts about theft should disappear.

We should consider: if we were among those three in the cave, which of our deeds would we have chosen to intercede for us? If we have good deeds worthy of intercession, we must improve and increase them. If we do not have deeds worthy of intercession, we must make a stronger effort to earn God's pleasure.

---

[1] Bukhari, Adab, 86,; Tirmidhi Zuhd 64.

THE GREAT FLOOD

The people of Noah worshipped the stars in the sky. Then they made and named idols in honor of the stars. When Noah was sent to his people, he told them that they were on the path of destruction. He told them to worship the one God, and if they accepted faith, they would be forgiven for their sins.

For nine hundred years, Noah conveyed the truth to his nation, but his people mocked him. He was so tired of trying to convince them, that he almost lost hope. He pleaded with his Lord to judge among the people of his nation, and supplicated to God to save him and the few people who had accepted faith with these words:

> "My Lord! I have surely called my people night and day; but my call has only caused them to flee (from accepting the truth). And every time I have called them so that You may forgive them, they have thrust their fingers in their ears, and wrapped themselves up in their garments, and grown more obstinate and arrogant.
>
> "My Lord! They have disobeyed me and followed those whose wealth and children have increased them only in loss and self-ruin. They have made terrible schemes, and they have said: 'Do not ever abandon your deities; do not abandon Wadd, nor Suwa, nor Yaghuth, or Ya'uq, or Nasr!' Indeed,

they have led many astray. (O God) increase not
these wrongdoers in anything but further straying."

God accepted Noah's prayers. Through Gabriel, the
angel of revelation, God commanded Noah to construct
an ark. A long journey awaited Noah and those who had
accepted faith. Immediately he began to build the ship in
accordance with the instructions revealed by Gabriel. In
the meantime, the people continued to mock him as they
passed by. Noah resisted their cruel words with immense
patience, and warned them of the grave punishment that
was to befall them.

Time passed, and the construction of the ship was
completed. As soon as Noah received the divine sign, the
believers and a pair of every species of animals, male and
female, boarded the ship. Then the doors to the ship were
closed. A horrifying downpour of rain began, and water
gushed up through gaps in the ground. The people struggled to escape from the rising water, but their attempts
were in vain. Houses were buried in the flood, and innumerous bodies floated on the surface.

As the ship floated on the rising waves, Noah noticed
a young man struggling to climb up onto the rocks. He
suddenly realized the young man was his own son, and
he called out in compassion:

"Embark with us, my son, and do not be with the
unbelievers!"

His son turned to him and said:

"I will take myself to a mountain that will protect me from the waters!"

Noah replied:

"Today there is no protection from God's judgment, except for him on whom He has mercy."

Noah's son was heedless to his father's words. Suddenly the waves came between them, and his son drowned.

The rains continued for a long time. At God's command, the rain ceased, the waters retreated, and the ship settled on a mountain peak. Noah and the believers had completed their journey. A life in which they could worship and live in accordance with the Lord's commandments awaited them.

Reflections

God created mankind, but never left them unsupervised. He sent messengers from among their own people, to teach them the true meaning of their existence. Prophets conveyed the truth to their nations, and guided them to faith. However, some of these nations abused the Prophets, and persisted in rejecting God and straying from the true path. Therefore God punished them.

For his entire life, Noah conveyed the truth, but was rejected and persecuted. Only a few of his people believed. Eventually, conditions became so bad that Noah raised his hands up in supplication to his Lord. Admitting defeat, he pleaded to his Lord for help against the rejecters of faith. Naturally, the supplication of such a messenger was not rejected by God. The Qur'an explains the event in a detailed manner:

> Before them, the people of Noah denied: they denied Our servant, and said: "This is a man possessed!" and he was rebuked (with insolence and prevented from preaching). So he prayed to his Lord, saying:
>
> "I have been overcome, so help me!" So We opened the gates of the sky, with water outpouring; And We caused the earth to gush forth with springs, so the waters (of the sky and the earth) combined for (the fulfillment of) a matter already ordained. And We carried him on a (construction of) wooden planks and nails, Running (through the water) under Our Eyes as a reward for one who had (wrongfully) been rejected with ingratitude. And indeed We left it (the Ark) as a sign (of the truth), then is there any that remembers and takes heed? But see how (severe) was My punishment and (how true) My warnings! (Qamar 54:9-16)

Noah, granted the crown of prophethood, was the servant of God, not humans, and he called his nation to God. His people called him crazy, which actually indicates the perfection of the Prophet's faith. In his society, all human values had disappeared. To their immoderate and unbalanced lifestyle, a Prophet would appear extreme to them. This dignified Messenger of God was trying to rebuild a society that had fallen into corruption. It was only natural for such a pious person to be labeled as "insane" by these misguided ones.

In the Qur'an, following the verses about the drowning of Noah's nation and the believers who were protected in a ship, it is asked: "Then, is there any that remembers and takes heed?" Here, I would like to add: is there any to take heed at Sodom and Gomorrah? There are many more places on earth where ruins are a sign of the fate of a corrupt nation. Each is revealed to us as clear as the verses of the Qur'an. Are there any people who learn a lesson from these examples of warning?

Even being the son of a Prophet is not a guarantee to enter the circle of faith. The most valuable people, in the eyes of God, are those who are closest to Him. When a human chooses to live a life distant from God, no matter who they are, God does not grant them faith.

THE MONEYLENDER

In ancient times there lived a man called Kifl. Kifl did not consider morals and values important, a wealthy man who could justify any means of earning money. Those in need came to him, but he would give them money only if they would repay him at a high rate of interest. When the date for the repayments came and people were unable to pay, he increased the rate of interest higher. If they were still unable to pay, he ordered his men to seize all their assets.

One day a woman came to ask for a loan. She was a respectable widow, and a mother totally devoted to her children. She had managed to live for a while on the money left to her by her husband, and then had tried to find work. But it was hard for a widow to find decent work outside, and she was afraid of being harassed.

The woman had an idea: she had learned how to weave carpets and this could be a way to work at home. But she needed a carpet loom, so she sought a loan to one. None of her friends or family had any money to loan to her. Sad and desperate, as she was walking home, she overheard a conversation about a moneylender in the city called Kifl, and she decided to visit him.

Kifl was very attracted to the woman he saw standing at his door. Realizing she was a widow without protection, Kifl made an indecent proposal: if she stayed with him for the night, he would give her the money and not expect repayment. The woman rejected his proposal with fury and got out immediately. She held up her hands in supplication and pleaded, "O Lord! Help me!"

Several days passed, and there was no food left at home. As her children cried with hunger, tears rolled down the poor woman's cheeks. She was desperate, and for the sake of her children, felt compelled to return to Kifl's house. She pleaded: "O Lord, forgive me! I will never commit such a sin again."

When Kifl opened the door, he gave her a wicked grin. The woman started crying and trembling. Kifl asked her why she was in such a state. She replied:

"I did not come here voluntarily. I have never in my life committed such a sin, and this is why I feel ashamed and afraid of God. I have been driven to sin due to poverty."

Kifl was touched, and his ruthless heart suddenly felt a pang of compassion. His entire soul felt embraced by a sense of remorse. Then words of repentance poured from his lips:

"Your poverty has forced you into committing a sin, but although God has blessed me with all this wealth, I have no hesitation or shame when I sin. I am the one who should be ashamed and fear God, not you."

His regret made him abstain from this sin. His heart became overwhelmed by contentment and joy. Kifl gave the widow money, and sent her home. She returned home rejoicing and glorifying her Lord for protecting her from evil.

Kifl became a different man. He pleaded for forgiveness for his previous sins. Although it was still early in the day, Kifl closed his shop and headed home. He raised his hands towards the heavens in supplication, and continued to plead forgiveness from his Lord all night until the early hours of the morning. That very night was Kifl's appointed time of death, and in this state of remorse and prayer, he submitted his soul to the Almighty.

Realizing that Kifl had not left home the next day, several of his friends went to his house. As they opened the door they found Kifl's dead body lying on the ground. There was a sign on the door: "God forgave Kifl for his sins."

The people were astonished. God had told the Prophet by divine revelation of the event and the means of Kifl's forgiveness. By his death, the people were taught a tremendous lesson.

Reflections

The gates to repentance are open to all people, at all times. However great the sin may be, when a person turns to his Creator in a state of repentance and sincerity, God accepts the person's pleas of remorse and forgives him.

God loves His servants who strive to earn His pleasure. With compassion, God sometimes prevents His servants from committing sin. It is the servant's duty to maintain a sound relationship with his Creator at all times.

THE DESOLATE VALLEY

Prophet Abraham, who was unable to have children with his first wife Sarah, married Hajar, who later gave birth to a son called Ishmael. Abraham's dear wife Sarah was overjoyed when she heard the news of the birth, but over a period of time, began to show signs of jealously. Even though her mind resisted this unfounded envy, her emotions rebelled.

In accordance with the divine command, Abraham took Hajar and Ishmael, who was newly weaned from his mother's milk, and set out on a journey. Although the evident reason for the migration was the jealousy between the wives, the sad mother and innocent baby were actually to succumb to their decree of fate— to lay the foundation for "the most precious fruit of the tree of humanity" centuries later. After a long and tiring journey, they eventually reached Mecca. In those days, Mecca was a place surrounded with sun burnt mountains, and black figures of rocks, a valley that made the soul shiver, a place where no crops grew and no caravans passed.

Leaving them only a water-skin and a few dates, this friend of God abandoned the two migrants in the desolate valley. In a separation that persecuted his soul, he set off for Damascus with tears rolling down his cheeks.

Resisting the temptation to look at them one last time, he walked off hastily, trying to disappear from sight as quickly as possible. Although Hajar called out to him several times: "Abraham! Abraham!" he was unable to answer. Due to his overpowering love and compassion, he was afraid of not having the strength to abandon the two sources of happiness in his life, his wife and child, and therefore defying the divine command. The moment the grieved woman managed to cease sobbing, she called out one more time:

"O Abraham, to whom are you entrusting us? Or is this a command from the Lord?"

Without turning around, the only words Prophet Abraham said were:

"Yes, this is the command of the Lord."

At this, Hajar commanded her tears to cease, and she called out once more:

"O Abraham, go! If this is the command of God, He will not abandon us, or allow any harm to befall us."

A child and a desperate woman were alone amidst the scorched, rugged mountains and rocks in the depths of this distant valley. What was going to happen now that they had no water and no shelter, and they were alone? They needed water, milk for the baby, companionship, protection, a guardian, or even a friend, a feeble aid. But was this not God's command? Did He not order this migration? Was this separation, this temporary seclusion not His wish? Therefore trust and total submission were necessary.

Hajar, enduring this migration in response to the divine command, submitted herself to her Creator. Leaving behind her life in the city, she endured the difficulties of settling in this dry, desolate valley, because this was the command of God. With faith, Hajar ignored her emotions, and sought refuge in the Lord. She had great affection for God; she was totally devoted to Him and placed her complete trust in Him alone.

But she could not just sit and wait for a miracle to happen while her baby was crying from hunger. She could not accept that submission was to sit there waiting without making any effort. She entrusted her child to God. Affirming her deep faith, she ran back and forth between Safa and Marwa, searching for a solution. Suddenly, unexpectedly, by God's mercy, the divine blessing appeared.

Water flowed from beneath Ishmael's feet from a ditch dug by the wing of an Angel. In this rocky desert, the spring was gushing with such force that the elated mother began to cry out in joy "Zam, zam!" According to reports, "Zam, zam!" in the language of that period, meant, "Stop, stop!"

Because of the Zamzam spring, Hajar quenched her thirst and appeased her hunger; she was able to nurse and raise her child. Soon after, God the Almighty sent a group of travelers from Yemen's Jurhum tribe toward the site in Mecca where the Kabah is today. Seeing the Zamzam spring, the travelers decided to settle there, and Hajar and Ishmael's desolation came to an end. Centuries later, a holy birth would take place here, the place where Hajar cried out to her Lord.

Reflections

People must endure and submit to the commands of God, regardless of the difficulties they may face. We must love and totally submit our souls to Him, and place our trust in Him alone. However, placing our trust in God does not mean expecting a result without making an effort. A person should always place his trust in God and do everything necessary to achieve a result. This is one of the commands of God.

THE CLOUD THAT WATERED
YUSUF'S GARDEN

A man had been walking for hours, and became very exhausted. The sun had reached its peak, exposing its full heat. He wanted to find a shady place to rest for a while. There was another day's journey ahead.

In the distance, he noticed a few trees. So he walked to them, and laid down in their shade. He was so tired that he fell asleep almost immediately. After a while, he heard a voice from nowhere saying, "Water Yusuf's garden!" Startled by the voice, he woke up, and thought, "It must have been a dream." As he was about to doze off again, he heard the same voice, and looked around to see where it was coming from. The voice was coming from above. When he raised his head, he saw a cloud full of rain. He was very surprised. Where did this cloud come from on such a sunny day? Whose voice was it? Who is Yusuf? In astonishment and fear, he decided to follow the cloud, to solve the intriguing matter.

He began to follow the cloud. Once again, a mysterious voice from nowhere commanded the cloud to water Yusuf's garden. Passing over a hill, the cloud emptied the rain it was carrying on the land beyond the hill. As he climbed the hill, he noticed a man working in a garden. He greeted the man and began talking. Sure enough, his name was Yusuf. But what had he done to deserve this special favor of the Lord?

The man explained in detail what had happened, and Yusuf replied:

"Come and sit down have something to eat and drink, and then I will tell you how this happened."

The man ate until he was sated, and to resolve his curiosity, Yusuf told his story.

"I have worked in this garden for years. I sow, harvest and earn my living from this garden. But I am extremely sensitive about one particular thing. I divide the produce from my garden into three. The first I give to the poor and people like yourself who pass here while travelling, the second I enjoy together with my family, and I store the remainder of the produce to sow again in this garden the next season. The man understood the mystery. God was pleased that Yusuf shared his produce with others, and his contribution of one-third of his wealth to charity was the reason for Yusuf being granted the favor of God.

Reflections

In the report of this incident in *Sahih al-Muslim*, the name of the man in question is not given. As one of the principles commanded by God, a believer should constantly be a generous giver. Since everything comes from

God, the believer must use a portion of his wealth to ensure that others live in peace and comfort.

Charity is the distribution of a believer's wealth for the sake of God. Because of charity, transient, worldly wealth becomes eternal, an important investment for the Hereafter. Giving charity has been conveyed, and mentioned in verses of the Qur'an and the traditions of the Prophet, as the sign of a believer. Indeed, this verse of the Qur'an affirms this: "You will never be able to attain godliness and virtue until you spend of what you love" (Al-Imran 3:92).

Wealth given in charity for the sake of God gives eternal reward. Referring to the chapter "Takaathur" (Rivalry in worldly increase) in the Qur'an, the Prophet marks this topic with the words: "the son of Adam says, 'my wealth, my wealth!'" But do you get anything (of benefit) from your wealth except for that which you ate and you finished it, or that which you clothed yourself with and you wore it out, or that which you gave as charity and you have spent it."[2]

It is possible to transform your wealth in this mortal world into capital for the Hereafter by distributing the necessary amount on earth to those in need. As a person who gives charity for the sake of God earns respect and from his society, and is also embraced by the protection of divinity. In another report of the Prophet, he tells us that two angels descend to earth every day, and whilst one of these angels supplicates for the increase of the wealth of

---

[2]   Muslim, Zuhd, 3;Tirmidhi, Zuhd 31.

those who give in charity, the other pleads for the wealth of the greedy and jealous to be destroyed.[3] The Prophet's words to his wife Hafsah are very striking: "Give in charity, be generous and give regularly. Do not withhold anything from your charity, and never accumulate excess possessions in greed, or God will withhold from you."[4]

---

[3] Bukhari, Zakah, 37; Musnad, 6/306, 347.
[4] Tirmidhi, Zuhd, 17; Musnad, 4/231.

THE FRUIT OF PATIENCE

Prophet Job (Ayyub) was a very rich man. He possessed substantial wealth, huge farms, numerous animals, and a large family. Despite all his wealth, he never displayed signs of conceit. He continued to worship God, and called others to the path of truth.

In the Qur'an, God portrayed Prophet Job as an example of patience and submission for humanity. He was subjected to an extensive trial. Initially he lost all his wealth, and then his children. He faced great financial and emotional difficulties, but despite these tribulations he never complained; to the contrary, he reacted with patience and praise.

Then God inflicted Prophet Job with a serious illness. Still he remained patient, and continued his duty of servitude. Throughout these tests, Prophet Job's wife stood by him, and gave him support.

Over time, God increased the severity of his illness. At one point, this great Prophet was incapable even of fulfilling his duty of worship, and was barely able to pray to God from his heart. It worried and grieved him. If he was unable to fulfill his worship of God, then what was the point in living? Therefore he raised his hands up in supplication to his Creator and pleaded:

"Truly, affliction has visited me and this is preventing me from fulfilling my duty of worship with my heart and my tongue. I cannot continue without worship. You are the Most Merciful of the merciful."

He performed this supplication not to regain his health and comfort, but because he longed to worship God. The Creator accepted the Prophet's prayer and told him to strike the ground with his foot, and to drink and bathe in the water that would appear from a spring beneath the ground. Prophet Job did exactly as he was commanded, and regained his health entirely. He was granted wealth greater than before, and blessed with even more children. He was given a life wealthier, more prosperous, healthier and more peaceful than ever before.

Time passed, and one day while Prophet Job was bathing, a swarm of gold locusts fell down from above. He immediately began to collect the locusts from the ground. Then God asked him:

"O Job! Have I not granted you a greater wealth than before? Why do you need to collect these?"

Prophet Job replied:

"Yes, my Lord! You have blessed me with great wealth. But this does not mean that I should ignore more prosperity from You. I accept whatever You grant me, because You are the Provider. How could I possibly reject anything that You give?"

Reflections

Every moment of life has various trials. If these tests are accepted with patience and fortitude, this matures a person and, according to his good intentions, brings him closer to his Lord. In the various stages of human life, trials and experiences teach us what a great blessing it is to live and to be healthy. Illness is undesirable and it befalls the just and the unjust, however, when illness occurs we must be patient.

The earth is the field of preparation for eternal life, the place of trial and achievement. Indeed, our lives on earth will come to an end one day, due to illness, a tragedy, disaster, or by any other means, and this time of death is determined at the moment of birth. As birth is, so one's departure from earth is also predestined. True life, is the life of the Hereafter. Therefore, when disaster befalls a person of faith, he should not only accept it with patience, saying, "this is atonement for my sins," he should also accept it with praise.

There is no objection in enjoying or desiring that which God has deemed lawful. Religion does not forbid owning possessions or wealth, but it forbids forgetting or ignoring God in the ambition of becoming rich. Islamic faith requires us to bear in mind that the true owner of all wealth is God, and that we should do not delay or ignore religious duties such as giving charity and alms.

This hadith of the Prophet corresponds excellently with the lessons to be learned from the story: "How

wonderful is the case of the believer! There is good for
him in everything, and this is not the case with anyone
but the believer. If he gains prosperity he praises God,
and this is good for him; and when affliction befalls
him, he endures it with patience, and that is also good
for him."[5]

---

[5]   Muslim, Zuhd 64.

THE MYSTERIOUS GUEST

Prophet Abraham traveled to Mecca to visit Ishmael, a beloved son that he had not seen for many years. Ishmael was greatly admired and loved by the locals. When Prophet Abraham reached Mecca, he asked the first person he saw where his son lived. The man gave him directions to his son's house, and when Prophet Abraham reached the house the man described, he knocked on the door. A miserable looking woman opened the door. Prophet Ishmael's wife was a very difficult, bad-tempered woman, and by no means deserved him for a husband. He was patient and tried very hard to change her aggressive ways, but his efforts were in vain. She was so stubborn and set in her ways that it was impossible to change her.

"Is Ishmael at home?" Prophet Abraham asked.

"No! He has gone to work," the woman replied harshly.

"How is your situation financially, can you manage on his earnings?" Prophet Abraham asked.

"No! It is very difficult, we can barely manage on what he earns," she complained.

"When Ishmael comes home, tell him that an old man sends his greetings. And by the way, can you remind him to renew his doorstep?"

And he left.

When Prophet Ishmael came home, a beautiful scent had spread around the entire house, and he realized that his father had visited. He was very excited, but there was nobody home except his wife.

"Did anyone visit you today?" he asked.

"Yes, a strange old man came and asked for you," his wife replied. "I told him that you were not at home, then he asked if we could manage on what you earn. I told him that things were difficult, and that we could barely get by on your earnings. Oh, I almost forgot, as he was leaving he said, "Remind your husband to renew his doorstep.""

Ishmael understood. He realized from his father's words that his wife was not a dutiful or kind person, and that divorcing her would be the right decision. The situation between Ishmael and his wife had become unbearable. There was no point in continuing the marriage, so Ishmael divorced her and later married another woman.

Time passed, and Prophet Abraham once again visited his son. In Mecca, he knocked on the door of his son's house. This time, a different woman opened the door.

"Is Ishmael home? I want to speak to him if it is possible," his father said.

"Ishmael is not at home at the moment. I am his wife. He has gone to the bazaar to sell his wares," the woman replied.

Prophet Abraham noticed the woman's polite, mature manner.

"How do you make a living, do you earn enough money to get by?" he asked.

"All praise to God. We live a life of prosperity. We can never thank the Lord enough for the blessings He gives us," she said. "I can see that you have traveled a long distance. I will bring you some food, and you can rest for a while. Wait here, I will be back soon."

Though Ishmael's wife had no idea that the man was her father in-law, she brought him something to eat. Prophet Abraham ate and prayed to the Lord.

"May the Lord bless you," he said. "I must leave now. When your husband comes home, tell him to retain his doorstep."

Shortly after, Abraham set out on his journey home. A couple of hours later, Ishmael returned home a couple of hours later. Before he even reached the door, he caught a hint of a beautiful fragrance, undoubtedly the scent of his father.

"Did any visitors come today?" he asked.

"Yes, an old man came and asked for you. I told him that you were not at home. Then he asked if we had any problems, if we were earning enough money to get by. I told him that we were comfortable, and that we lived in prosperity. I gave him some food, and just as he was leaving he said to me, 'Give your husband my greetings, and tell him to retain his doorstep.' I did not understand what he meant by this; do you have any idea what he meant?"

"My dear wife! That old man was my father, and you are my doorstep," Ishmael explained. "He warned me to treat you well, to be good to you, and not upset you in any way. This means that my father liked you, and was pleased with the way you treated him."

Reflections

People should welcome guests politely, serve and treat them with kindness. In one of the traditions of the Prophet, it states that a person who believes in God and the Last Day should show hospitality to his guest. A grim, sulky face and actions portraying displeasure will make guests uncomfortable, so a believer must avoid such actions.

Every parent wants the best for their children, and wishes no harm to befall them. Parents warn and advise their children when they are concerned. If the parent's demands comply with Islam, it is the son or daughter's duty to fulfill these requests. If a person earns the approval of his parents and obeys God, he will never be led astray.

CAN TWO SILVER COINS BE MORE VALUABLE THAN A POUCH OF GOLD?

God sent one of His angels disguised as a very poor man wearing torn, worn out clothing to test two men in the same city, one the wealthiest and the other the poorest. The angel went first to the poor man's house. Although he was very poor, he was a humble, grateful man, and when he saw a ragged, untidy person standing before him, he asked:

"Welcome, how can I help you?"

"Sorry to trouble you," the angel said. "I am traveling, but I have no means to continue. I need money in order to continue my journey home."

The poor man had two silver coins in his pocket. He gave one of the coins to the traveler, and said:

"This is all the money I have. If I had more, believe me I would give you more. Take this and use it on your journey."

The angel said:

"May the Creator be eternally pleased with you. This is more than enough; I was not even expecting this much. I can see that you are poor. Indeed, I am very touched that you gave me half of your money. Give me your blessings."

The angel left, and went to the wealthiest man in the city. The rich man had invited distinguished residents of the city to his home, and was talking with them. The angel, disguised as a poor man, knocked on the door and walked in. He explained his situation, and asked for help. The rich man turned to the mufti of the city, who was among his guests, and said:

"I am tired of these people. Every day so many people just like him come to my door and ask for money. Although I never send any of them away empty-handed, to tell you the truth, I do get quite annoyed."

The mufti replied:

"This may be so, but give for the sake of God, so that God will return this favor to you. There is reward in everything you do for the sake of God."

The rich man said:

"Okay, you have made your point. I am constantly giving charity to these people anyway."

So the rich man took a pouch of gold coins from his pocket. As he was handing the pouch over to the poor man, he boasted:

"Beggar, take this! I hope you realize that nobody around here would ever give you as much money as me."

The angel was disgusted by the rich man's attitude, and was grieved, for God was the One who granted this man his wealth, and after all, he was supposedly giving alms for the sake of God. But this was not the way to give charity to others.

Then the mufti spoke, to teach a lesson to the rich man and all those present:

"Your attitude is entirely wrong. Expecting gratitude, or taunting the poor, can reduce or even eliminate the divine reward for charity. Be sincere in giving, and when you give, give from the heart. Never forget that when you give, you are giving to the Creator, and He will give you much more in return."

The poor man had passed his test; God was pleased with his actions, for he gave charity with sincerity, and without conceit. But the rich's man's alms had no value in the eyes of God, and two silver coins became more profitable than a pouch full of gold.

Reflections

Giving is a moral duty commanded by God. Our Creator bestowed us with many blessings, from the air we breathe to the food we eat, and He continues to provide unconditionally. At the same time, the Creator demands generosity from His servants in the Qur'an:

> And spend (in God's cause and for the needy) out of whatever We provide for you before death comes… (Al-Munafiqun 63:10).

It is the servant's duty to distribute blessings from God to those in need. A person must perform this duty without offending the opposite party. In fact, it is stated in a hadith that the left hand should not see what the right hand gives in charity. Money and wealth given in charity does not belong to the individual, it belongs to those in need — the provider of charity is merely returning his debt.

> O you who believe! Render not vain your almsgiving by putting (the receiver) under an obligation and taunting – like him who spends his wealth to show off to people and be praised by them, and believes not in God and the Last Day. (Baqarah 2:264)

Charity forms a bridge in communities between the extremes of wealth and poverty, encourages humility and brotherhood for the rich, and protects the poor from indigence and oppression. In the past, some considerate believers discreetly placed pouches full of gold in places where they could be found by the needy, thus protecting the poor from embarrassment by not giving the charity personally.

Charity given to the poor must never be underestimated, for God considers the sincerity of one's intention, not the amount one gives. The Prophet said that Muslims should save themselves from the hellfire, even if the charity is just half a date. Among the Companions, there was a courageous man called Abu Aqil, one of the most honored residents of Medina. Despite his own poverty, Abu Aqil gave his possessions to the Prophet to distribute to the poor, and was ill-treated and reviled by the Hypocrites. Ignoring them, he continued to roam the bazaars of Medina with a rope around his neck, earning a living by carrying loads from one place to another. He would earn four or five coins a day, and gave half to the poor, and half to the Prophet. In an attempt to create animosity between Abu Aqil and the people, the hypocrites said, "God is in no need of his charity!" to make him the target of criticism.[6]

Indicating their evil actions, and complimenting Abu Aqil on his behavior, the Qur'an says:

> They taunt the believers, who give for God's sake more than they are duty-bound to give, as well as those who can find nothing to give except their hard toil, and they scoff at them. God causes their scoffing to rebound on themselves, and for them is a painful punishment. (Tawbah 9:79)

When Abu Aqil carried loads around the bazaars, he gave generously and fulfilled his duty. Indeed, he will reap the rewards for his actions in the Hereafter.

In a hadith, the Prophet emphasizes the anguish we earn when we remind others of our own generosity: "There are three classes (of people) to whom God will not speak on the Day of Judgment nor will He look at them or redeem them: Those who trail their robes (arrogant ones), those who put others under obligation by mentioning the favor they made to them and those who try to market their goods by false swearing."[7]

"A kind word and forgiving are better than almsgiving followed by taunting. God is All-Wealthy and Self-Sufficient, (absolutely independent of the charity of people), All-Clement (Who shows no haste in punishing.)" (Al-Baqarah 2:263)

---

6   See: Ibn Kathir, Tafsir, 4/125
7   Muslim, Iman, 171-174.

THE KING FROZE

Prophet Abraham set out on a journey with his wife, Sarah. In order to reach their destination, they had to pass through the land of a cruel king. The king had a very bad reputation: he abducted beautiful married women by using force against their husbands and kept them in his palace. Abraham had heard about the king and his evil actions. Before they entered the city, Abraham told his wife:

"There is a cruel king who rules these lands. He takes beautiful women by force from their husbands. If he realizes that you are my wife, he may try to abduct you. If he speaks to you and asks who I am, tell him that I am your brother. Indeed, this is not a lie, for we are all brothers and sisters in faith."

As Sarah passed through the city center, the king's men noticed her. Although Prophet Abraham put up a great struggle to protect her, he was unable to resist the king's men, who were armed, and powerful in strength and number. The only thing he could do was pray to God. So raising his hands up towards the heavens, he prayed for the Lord to protect his dear wife. The men took Sarah to the palace to please their king. On the way, she supplicated to God:

"O God! I believe in You and Your messenger, Abraham. Throughout my whole life I have protected my honor. I am pleading with You, O Lord, to keep this cruel man away from me, guard me from his evil, and grant me protection."

The guards escorted Sarah to the king. When the king saw her, he wanted desperately to touch her. But as he reached his hand out toward Prophet Abraham's wife, suddenly the king's arm and his entire body froze. No matter how much he tried, he was unable to move. In desperation, he began to plea:

"I have no idea what you have done to me, but you are the only one who can save me. Do something; help me! I promise that I will not try to touch you again, and as soon as I recover, I will set you free."

So Sarah prayed again to God, and the king regained his senses. But breaking his promise, the king reached out again to touch her. Again, the king's body froze completely. And again, he pleaded for help. The king recovered again because of Sarah's prayer and stubbornly attempted to touch her for the third time. But when he froze again, and the king finally realized that he would never be able to touch her, he summoned his guards and ordered:

"Get this woman away from me immediately! You have not brought me a human, you have brought me a demon. Bring the servant woman, Hajar, and escort them both away from here, I forbid you to bring women like that to my palace again."

Upon his command, the king's guards took Sarah and Hajar to Prophet Abraham and ordered them to leave the land immediately. Prophet Abraham was very surprised to see his wife approaching with another woman. On one hand he was grateful to God for returning his wife safely. On the other hand, he was concerned about what had happened at the palace.

Sarah explained everything to him, and added:

"All praise to the Lord! He protected me from the evil of this cruel king. He left the king devastated, and granted me this servant girl."

Hajar later became the second wife of Prophet Ibrahim, and the mother of Ishmael, his firstborn son.

Reflections

This is a world of trials. Every individual's trial varies according to their strength, and their value in the eyes of God. A believer possesses two weapons to deal with trials: patience and prayer. Patience and prayer eliminates all kinds of affliction. Indeed, God never grants His servant a burden greater than he can bear.

God accepts the supplications of those who turn to Him in sincerity, and does not abandon them. A believer should turn to Him in prayer not only during times of difficulty, but also in times of prosperity, and never straying from the path of divinity.

Breaking a promise is disliked by God. According to Prophet Muhammad, peace and blessings be upon him, it is one of the signs of hypocrisy. A believer must never break promises.

THE CAT THAT WAS LEFT TO DIE

L ong ago, there lived a woman who was addicted to cleaning. She cleaned her home continuously from early in the morning until late at night. If she saw a tiny speck of dust anywhere in the house, she would lose her temper and become hysterical. Her obsession with cleanliness had made the woman a nervous wreck. She made the lives of those around her miserable.

The woman's children were tired of her behavior. They were beaten on many occasions just for playing indoors. The children considered their home a prison.

While their mother was out one day, the children found a kitten in the street. The tiny animal was very hungry, and shaking from the cold. Their mother was very strict regarding animals. They had asked if they could keep a cat at home before, but their mother had refused angrily.

The children decided to take the kitten home, feed and play with it for awhile and then sneak it back out without their mother seeing. The kitten finished all the food almost immediately, and then began to play with the children. The children were enjoying themselves so much that time flew by. They did not realize how late it was, and the house became untidy.

Suddenly realizing that their mother would be home soon, the eldest child told the others to take the kitten out of the house. Their mother would be very angry if she saw the house in such a state, so they had to clean before she returned.

Just then the front door opened, and the children's mother walked in. As she looked around at the mess, she became hysterical with anger. She shouted and screamed, picking up anything she could find and throwing it at her children. Then she noticed the tiny kitten.

"So you brought a cat home without my permission. I will show you all, don't worry. Go to your room immediately, you are all forbidden to leave the house indefinitely."

She grabbed the kitten by the scruff of its neck, and threw it down into the storeroom. Then she locked the door, and shouted in anger:

"I am locking the cat in this room. I have hidden the key. As your punishment, the cat is staying in there until it dies from hunger and thirst. If any of you even attempt to release it, I will make life in this house hell!"

The children were terrified to leave their room. The poor kitten cried continuously. The weak whimpers of the little creature had no effect on the cruel, coldblooded woman. She called out:

"Serves you right! You are going to remain in there until you die."

Days passed, and the kitten's cries ceased. The kitten had died, and its stench had spread from the storeroom throughout the entire house. The woman callously threw its body into the outside dustbin.

The woman's actions angered God, Who has infinite compassion for every creature He made. God ordained Hell as her punishment. For killing a kitten, the woman would suffer the consequences there.

Reflections

As it is a believer's duty to be compassionate to humans, he must be merciful to animals. In the example of the Prophet, we see great empathy for animals. On his journey home from a battle, the Prophet and the Companions stopped to rest. Noticing a bird's nest nearby, some of the Companions took baby chicks out of their nest to hold. Then the mother bird appeared, and began to fly around in distress, beating her wings violently. The Prophet became angry at the suffering his Companions had caused the mother bird, and ordered them to return the chicks to their nest. A believer should show compassion to every creature on earth because "those who have no mercy will be shown no mercy."

A mother should not deprive her children from play because it will disrupt the tidiness of the home. A certain area of the home should be allocated for children to play.

Obsessive cleanliness — indeed, excessive behavior of any kind — is disliked by God. In a hadith, the Prophet said that those who demonstrate excessiveness were subject to destruction. Then he remarked: "The best of dealings are those performed in moderation."

SWALLOWED BY A WHALE

P rophet Jonah, peace be upon him, was born in Nineveh, the capital of Assyria and an important center for trade, and was sent to his people as a messenger. For years Prophet Jonah called the people of Nineveh, a nation of idol-worshipers living in prosperity and comfort, to believe and worship one God. His nation not only rejected his message, but also taunted, abused and oppressed him. Ignoring their abuse, Jonah continued to call them to the religion of truth.

Eventually, he began to lose hope that his nation, which persisted in mocking him despite his sincerity, would find the true path. Despite his years of effort, there was no sign of remorse in the souls of his people. Having sensed that God's punishment was near, he decided to migrate. Before he moved, Prophet Jonah went to his people one last time, and told them that a great punishment would befall them. He said the first signs of the punishment would be that their faces would change color and become deformed.

When Prophet Jonah sensed that God's punishment was near, he left the city without being ordered to do so. His migration was a premature withdrawal from his people who stubbornly rejected faith.

With grief, Jonah set out on his journey. He abandoned Nineveh, the land of his birth, and near the Tigris River boarded a ship full of passengers. After sailing for a while, the ship inexplicably stopped in the middle of the sea. Everyone onboard was bewildered. No matter what they did, the ship refused to budge. A sudden squall made the situation grave — the ship was in danger of sinking. The passengers begin to panic, but a voice called out:

"The ship is not moving because there is a criminal onboard."

Everyone began to speculate about who the criminal was. Then a passenger suggested:

"We can put everyone's name in a basket, and leave God to determine who the criminal is. Whoever's name is pulled out of the basket, we will throw him overboard and be freed of this curse."

All the passengers agreed. The name drawn was Jonah. Everyone was surprised, because he had seemed like a trustworthy man; everything about his behavior was saintly. None of them believed that he could be a criminal. They decided to repeat the drawing, and again, his name was drawn. On the third drawing, the same name appeared. Accepting it as a trial from his Creator, Prophet Jonah declared, "I am the rebellious servant!"

Jonah was thrown overboard. It was late at night, and the storm made the waves violent. Prophet Jonah fell into the sea and struggled against the rough sea. There was no one to help him, no one to hear his cries. He was deserted, abandoned, and utterly alone. A short time later, he was swallowed by a whale. In the darkness of the night, the ocean and the whale collaborated against Jonah. He knew there was a power that could save him, One Who could overrule the darkness, the ocean and the whale. Undoubtedly, this power was the Creator of all motives and means, God the Almighty.

In the night, Prophet Jonah pleaded to his Lord: "O Lord! There is no god but You, glorified be You! Truly, I have been of the wrongdoers."

God accepted Jonah's sincere repentance, and commanded the whale to leave its guest safely on the shore. And with His grace and mercy, God commanded a marrow plant, which grows quickly and has wide leaves, to grow over Prophet Jonah. The plant covered him with shade, and protected him from flies, and Jonah remained under it until he recovered from his ordeal.

Meanwhile, just as Prophet Jonah had warned, the people of Nineveh awakened one morning to find that their faces had changed color. Looking up, they noticed a huge dark cloud approaching. A veil fell from their eyes, and the people realized that they had oppressed and abused a prophet of God. They came together and prayed, asking God for forgiveness. God accepted their supplications and forgave them. Prophet Jonah later returned to his people.

Reflections

The elimination of the punishment ordained for Prophet Jonah's people was likely a favor God granted only to that nation, as we have no record of it happening before or after this event.

Perhaps, as the signs of destruction appeared, a good deed at that instant induced the mercy of God. When the people of Prophet Jonah recognized the signs of punishment, they gathered together and turned to the Creator in sincere repentance; so God granted them a second chance to prepare for the Hereafter.

Normally, when God ordained a punishment for a nation, He commanded His messengers to abandon the region prior to it. But Prophet Jonah had decided to leave his people before God commanded him to. Perhaps God therefore lifted the nation's punishment and, rather like a lightning rod, the punishment was instead given to Prophet Jonah as an additional warning to his people.

Prayer is the weapon of a believer. A hadith states: "Only supplication (to God) can avert what is destined to befall." The hadith should be considered as an encouragement to use supplication, the means of growing closer to the Creator, as a form of protection against tribulation.

THE COMPANIONS OF THE CAVE

The Companions of the Cave (Ashab al-Kahf) were a group of young believers who had abandoning their faith-rejecting, idol-worshiping nation. They had fled from their city and taken shelter in a cave. Their story was to be an example of faith in the Hereafter, and a metaphor for resurrection after death. Their names were Yamliha, Maksalina, Mislina, Marnush, Dabarnush, Shazanush, Kafashtatayyush, and their dog was named Qitmir. The chapter Al-Kahf in the Qur'an tells the tale of these young men, who lived lives of wisdom and warning.

During the time of the Companions of the Cave, Christianity was on the decline and rulers were hedonists. A cruel, tyrannical king named Decius had become an idol worshiper. He persecuted followers of God and carried out genocide of those who believed in God's unity. But seven men in his palace believed and had faith. On hearing of them, Decius summoned the young men to this throne, and ordered them to renounce their faith on threat of death. But the young men said that worshiping a man-made idol was a sin, and refused to renounce their faith. Decius, afraid of repercussions within the palace, did not kill the young men right away.

The seven men felt that it was unsafe to remain any longer in the city. Worried they would be forced to abandon their faith, they chose to migrate in order to be free to practice their religion. A short distance from the city, the young men found shelter in a cave at the foot of a mountain, together with a dog that protected them on their journey. By the command of God, the men fell into a long, deep sleep. For three centuries, they remained sleeping undisturbed in the cave. During the epoch, their bodies were miraculously turned over from left to right, by the command of God, to protect them from sores and decay.

After they had migrated from the city, the young men had been forgotten. One day, they awakened in the late afternoon. Though three hundred years had passed, the young men felt as if they had slept for a day or two. They were hungry; choosing one of their number, they gave him money and sent him to the city to buy food for the rest. As he approached the city, Yamliha was astonished. Everything had changed — roads and surroundings were altered to be nearly unrecognizable. Centuries had passed since the death of Decius, the ruler who had persecuted the followers of Jesus in his time.

Yamliha went into a bakery to buy bread. The baker, suspicious of Yamliha's dated attire, looked at the ancient coins the young man had given him. Assuming he had found a hidden treasure, the baker complained to the ruling authority. The local authorities, after looking over this strange man buying food with coins over three hundred years old, escorted him to the king. Standing before the king, Yamliha explained the incident that occurred, he believed, one day earlier. But in the three hundred years that had passed, Christianity had triumphed over the hedonism and paganism which had been practiced. A society had emerged that believed in life after death. Listening to Yamliha's story, the kingdom became convinced that they were witnessing a miracle of God, and their faith became stronger. When Yamliha returned to the cave, he and his friends submitted their souls to God the Almighty.

Reflections

The Companions of the Cave abandoning their society to take refuge in a cave cannot be considered escape, because it was not due to fear or cowardice. The Companions of the Cave abandoning the city to take shelter in the cave is resembles the story of Umar, who went to the Kabah in broad daylight and said: "I am migrating to Medina; any of you who wish to make his wife a widow, and his children orphans, should come with me." This is the true meaning of migration. Indeed, the migration of the Companions of the Cave may have been a desertion, but it was a desertion that sought refuge in the Creator.

Their migration reflected the sincere belief of the young men, and succeeded in transforming the society. The courageous rebellion of the brave young men undoubtedly touched the souls of many of their people. Their beliefs and actions were conveyed from mouth to mouth, from soul to soul, and eventually caused the utter transformation of their nation. The incident was a seed that slowly developed, grew and flourished, and ultimately embraced the whole society.

It is reported that the Companions of the Cave were members of the palace. A person willingly abandoning the comfort and prosperity of the palace, and instead choosing a path that rebelled against the king, was unimaginable. Naturally, their choice attracted attention — enduring difficulties with total devotion for the sake of their faith had a ripple effect on the society. The people began to ponder the message that the men represented and conveyed.

The cave was an abode of inspiration, a place of self-discovery. In a hedonistic, polytheistic society, especially one that is powerful and unjust, only the determination of a Prophet could undermine, damage and eventually defeat the elites. Let us examine the life of Prophet Muhammad, peace and blessings be upon him, for a moment. Did he not spend six months in a cave in the early stages of his prophethood? Many of those who followed the path of the Prophet also spent a certain period of their lives in the seclusion of a cave: Imam Ghazzali, Imam Rabbani, Mawlana Khalid and Bediüzzaman Said Nursi spent time in seclusion to gain inspiration, discover the essence of life, and gather the energy they required to strive against disbelief and persecution. According to their piety and servitude, some of the great scholars of Islam remained in seclusion for five or ten years. There have even been those who remained in isolation for as long as sixty years. Indeed, a period of seclusion is necessary for a human to be endowed with certain divine attributes and adorned with divine inspiration.

Companions of the Cave struggled to protect their faith. They believed in their Creator, and God increased their faith and enhanced their hearts with spirituality and wisdom. When they migrated, there were probably no more than ten monotheists among their own people. Their society was very relentless towards those who believed in the unity of God; they forced them to renounce their faith or stoned them to death. Under such conditions, they had no choice but to abandon the city. In order to avoid being tempted from the path of faith or forced to practice polytheism, the young men hid in a cave in anticipation of God's compassion. Just as dying for God's sake in such situations is an honorable act, migrating for God's sake is a practice of equal virtue. The Companions of the Cave were powerless to transform their own society, and also had nowhere to go — there was no society like Medina's to migrate to. They had three choices: to become polytheists, die as martyrs, or migrate with the hope of God's mercy. The Creator had compassion upon the youths, and saved them from persecution. He also immortalized their memory, as an example for generations to come.

THE JOURNEY OF MOSES AND KHIDR

Musa, a prophet given knowledge and wisdom by God, told his people about God and faith, and guided them to the path of truth. One day a man from among his people asked Prophet Moses:

"O Moses! Who is the most learned among humans?"

Without hesitation, Moses replied: "I am the most learned of all humans!"

He was a prophet of God, and God had blessed him with outstanding knowledge. But there was someone more knowledgeable than he, and his name was Khidr. God said to Moses:

"At the meeting of the two seas is one of My righteous servants; he is more knowledgeable than you."

Moses became curious, and desperately wanted to meet Khidr and learn from him. He asked God where to find this man. God said:

"O Moses! Place a salted fish in a basket, and wherever the fish begins to jump and then disappears, this is where you will find My learned servant."

Preparing all the food and drink they would need, and the fish in the basket, Moses set out on the journey with his helper, Joshua. At the end of a day's tiring journey, when they reached the meeting of the two seas, it was almost dark. They rested by the shore for awhile, and the pair drifted off to sleep. In the meantime, the fish began to jump, higher and higher, until it leaped from the basket and into the sea. Joshua woke up and saw the fish disappear into the sea.

Later, when Moses awoke, Joshua forgot to tell him about the fish diving into the ocean. Gathering their possessions, the two continued on the journey. After they had walked for quite awhile, Moses began to feel hungry and asked Joshua to prepare the food. Joshua remembered the fish diving into the ocean, and apologizing, he told Moses. Prophet Moses replied:

"In that case, we most return immediately, for my Lord told me that this is where I was to meet the most learned of all men. We must return without wasting any more time."

When they reached the spot where the fish had dived into the sea, Prophet Moses noticed a stranger sitting on a rock. It was Al-Khidr. Greeting him, Prophet Moses said: "May I follow you so that you may teach me something of the knowledge of guidance which you have been taught? Al-Khidr replied:

"O Moses! You will not be able to tolerate traveling with me. You will find it difficult to comprehend certain things, and you will experience incidents that you won't understand. It will be impossible for you to tolerate. Indeed, there is knowledge and wisdom that God taught me alone, wisdom that you will never know. Perhaps it will be better for you if you return home.

Moses replied:

"By the power of God, you will see what a patient and tolerant man I really am."

Al-Khidr said:

"Very well, on one condition. You must never question what I do until I choose to explain my reasons, and you must not object to anything I do. Do you accept my terms?"

Prophet Moses accepted Al-Khidr's conditions, and they began the journey together. As they were about to board a ship, a bird flew over and landed immediately in front of them. Then the bird flew down near the waves and took a drop of water from the sea with its beak. Pointing at the bird, Al-Khidr told Moses:

"Look, Moses! You see the drop of water that bird took from the sea is like your knowledge and my knowledge combined, and the ocean is like the knowledge of God."

Al-Khidr had taught Moses his first lesson. Because the ship owners recognized Al-Khidr, they treated him with great kindness, even refusing to accept money for the journey. But after the ship began to sail, Al-Khidr made a hole in the floor of the ship. Water gushed through the hole, and the ship began to tilt to one side. Moses gasped in astonishment, wondering how he could do such an injustice against innocent people. He cried:

"What have you done? You are going to sink the ship! How could you do this to these kind people who even refused to accept money from you? Do you really want all these innocent people to drown?"

Al-Khidr replied:

"I warned you that you were to be patient and not object to or question anything I did."

Prophet Moses replied:

"I am sorry; for a moment I forgot the promise I made to you. I will not question anything you do from now on. If I do, you may end our friendship."

When they reached the port, they disembarked the ship together and continued their journey by foot. Suddenly a group of young children, who were running and playing, appeared before Al-Khidr and Moses. Al-Khidr pulled aside one of the young boys and killed him. Moses wanted to help the boy, but he was already dead. Turning to Al-Khidr angrily, he cried:

"How could you do such a thing? Why did you kill this young innocent child?"

Calmly, Al-Khidr replied:

"I warned you before that you would not be able to tolerate the things you see." Once again, Moses remembered his promise:

"I apologize. I broke my promise again. But this is that last time; I will not question you again. If I do, then you can end our friendship."

Al-Khidr gave Moses one more chance. They continued walking until they reached a village. Hungry, they asked the villagers for food, but none of the villagers welcomed them as guests. As they walked further into the village, they noticed a wall that was on the verge of collapsing. Al-Khidr repaired it with his bare hands. Once again, Moses was unable to resist his curiosity:

"These villagers refused to accept us as guests or even to give us food. Nevertheless, you repaired a collapsing wall of in their village. Are you going to ask them to pay you for repairing the wall?"

Al-Khidr replied:

"I told you that you would not be able tolerate this journey with me, and I warned you not to question anything I did. It is time for us to part and go our own ways."

It was the third time that Moses had violated his promise; no apologies or excuses were to be accepted.

Al-Khidr continued:

"Unfortunately, this is the end of our journey together, so now I will explain my reasons for the actions that you found so intolerable. Let's begin with the hole I made in the ship. I damaged it because there is a cruel king who is seizing every ship on our route that is in good condition, but when the king's men notice that the ship is damaged, they will allow it to continue. The ship is owned by a very poor family. By damaging the ship, I prevented the king from seizing the vessel that is their only means of income.

The ship's owners will repair the hole in the vessel and continue their journey.

"As for the child that I killed — his parents are God's beloved servants. If he grows up, the child would be the reason they stray from the path of the Almighty, and abandon their faith. God pitied the child's parents and decided to protect them from his evil. In his place, God will grant these devoted believers with a dutiful child.

"And finally, let me explain the wall I repaired. Hidden beneath the wall was a treasure that one of the villagers, a righteous man, had buried for his children to inherit. If the wall collapsed, the treasure would have been found and used by others, because the children are still very young. The Creator wanted the children to find the treasure when they grow up.

"You see, whatever I did was not of my own accord, but was the will and the command of God."

After telling this story, Prophet Muhammad, peace and blessings be upon him, added:

"May God bestow His mercy upon Moses! If he had remained patient, we would surely have heard more regarding the adventures of this journey."

Reflections

Some journeys must be performed more than once, just as some lessons must be learned over and over. Faithful believers must never be satisfied with materialistic knowledge alone, but must learn spiritual wisdom. Prophet

Moses and his helper learned to be disciplined, and became an example for this world's youth. The journey was a Sufi metaphor for becoming disciplined.

Every stage in a journey has specific restrictions, and the reasons for the restrictions are apparent only to the enlightened. During the era of righteousness, after the time of the Companions, believers traveled long distances on horseback with a passion for knowledge and wisdom. To achieve this today, we must behave with the same undeterred discipline as the believers of the past. Learning lessons will continue until the Last Day, and humans of all levels of understanding will perceive meaning according to their individual abilities.

The damaged ship was a symbol, a metaphor for the probable means of rescuing the innocent from cruel oppressors. In every era, it is a principle of believers to seek social justice, and the precept will continue until the Day of Judgment.

Another subtle point is conveyed in each of the three events. It is necessary for the mind and rationalism to surrender to the heart and spirituality. Kind people are rewarded by their ship being purposely damaged, an apparently innocent child is killed, and a crumbling wall in an inhospitable village is repaired. We discovered that logic fails at the gate to the world of wisdom. We are called to surrender to the spirituality of faith. To obtain the ability to perceive spiritual truths and wisdom, one must isolate themselves from others, and abstain from the pleasures of this world, and tirelessly work to progress on the divine, eternal path.

The merging of the two seas (Majma-ul-Bahrain), mentioned in various commentaries of the Qur'an, is used as a metaphor for the merging of the knowledge of Prophet Moses and Al-Khidr. One is a sea of evident knowledge, and the other is a sea of spiritual knowledge.

THE CHARITY GIVEN TO THREE
DIFFERENT PEOPLE

Long ago there lived a man called Murad* who, with his devoted worship and excellent manner, was an example to all who knew him. He was also a very generous man, who gave large amounts of charity to the poor.

One day, Murad went to the bazaar to buy provisions for his family. As he walked through the marketplace, he noticed a man sitting on the roadside. Known as a thief by the locals, no one spoke or showed kindness to him. Then to the astonishment of the traders and passersby, Murad took money from his pocket and gave it to the thief. Everyone was astonished.

"Did you see that? Murad must be so distracted, that he gave charity to a thief without even realizing."

But Murad knew what he had done.

He continued walking through the market, and noticed a trader selling apples. He asked for two kilos of apples, and as he was waiting, Murad saw a woman standing by the trader's stall. The woman was known for her indecent behavior, and was shunned by society. Again, Murad took money from his pocket and gave it to the woman. The witnesses were even more bewildered.

"There is definitely something wrong with Murad today, do you really think a woman like that deserves charity?"

Murad heard what people were saying, but he knew what he was doing. In his heart, he praised God's name.

Murad finished shopping, and was now on his way home. As he reached the end of the marketplace, he saw a man known to be very wealthy. Once again, he took some money from his pocket and gave it to the man. The people were confused, and could not resist asking any longer. They walked over to him and said:

> "Murad, I hope you do not mind us asking, but is there something wrong with you today? You gave charity to a thief, then to an indecent woman, and now you gave charity to a rich man who does not deserve charity. Do you think it is right to give charity to such people?"

Murad said:

> "Yes, you are right. I gave these three people charity. I gave charity to the thief in the hope that he may stop stealing, and I gave charity to the woman in the hope that she may abandon fornication, and I gave charity to the rich man in the hope that this may be a lesson to him, and that he, too, may give charity to others."

The people understood Murad, and apologized for misunderstanding him.

Reflections

Giving charity to the needy is a duty for those who have means. Indeed, charity itself is wisdom, portrayed clearly in a hadith of the Prophet:

"Charity is incumbent upon every Muslim."

One of the Companions asked: "O Messenger of God, what if a person has nothing to give?"

The Prophet replied: "He should work with his bare hands, for this will benefit himself, and give from his earnings to charity."

The Companion asked: "What if he is unable to do so?"

The Prophet replied: "He should help the poor and needy of the community."

When the Companion asked: "What if he is unable to do this?"

In response to the Companion's persistence, the Prophet said:

"He should do good deeds, and protect himself from evil. Indeed, this is a form of charity. A kind word and a smile, too, are among the vast boundaries of charity."[8]

Charity for those in need is necessary to form a bridge between the wealthy and the poor. Intention is the basis for judging the value and significance of deeds, from the most trivial to the greatest. There are even rewards to be earned from intentions alone. For example, if a person

---

8   Bukhari, Zakah, 30; Muslim, Zakah, 45-46; Nasai, Zakah 6.

intends to perform a good deed but does not, the individual is rewarded for the deed. If the person intends to as performs the good deed, according to the deed and conditions, sometimes he will be rewarded ten, one hundred and on some occasions even seven hundred times the reward of the deed. Mercifully, if an evil action is intended but not performed, no sin is recorded, but if the evil action is intended and carried out, only one sin is recorded. The man in the story gave charity with sincere intentions, earning a generous heavenly reward, and also intended to win, and won the hearts and minds of those who were not living lives of belief.

Customarily, it is important to ensure that charity is given to those truly in need or those defined by the Qur'an. Failing to give to the prescribed places or people means failing to give charity. The sole concession involves the giver's sincerity and belief in his choice; if the individual believes in his choice, then he has fulfilled his duty due to his sincerity of intention. But the most excellent charity reaches those in need. It is very important to know who is truly in need in society, so that charity reaches the most deserving people.

Although the people criticized Murad for giving alms first to the thief, then to an adulteress, and finally to a wealthy man, his aim of encouraging them to abandon stealing, fornication and greed was honorable and rational. Alms save the poor from being forgotten and transform them into individuals sought out by society. When charity foundations began to operate as organizations, as during the period of Umar ibn Abdulaziz, poverty was eliminated.

Charitable donations exceeded the need for the donations. In such an environment the needy are saved from pursuing the rich; instead the poor are sought by the wealthy.

The wealthy individual who wants to give alms will be rewarded for spending the wealth given to him by God, as it is the path decreed by the Creator.

---

* The character in this story was referred to only as "a person of the children of Israel" in a hadith of the Prophet. We referred to the character by the name of Murad.

THE BLAZING FIRE

When we look at the life of Prophet Abraham, we see that migration played an important role. He was "a figure of migration." According to historical records, astrologers stated that in the year of Prophet Abraham's birth, a child would come into the world who was to transform the faith of the people and end the reign of King Nimrod. Nimrod ordered the killing of every male infant who was born. So Azar, the father of Abraham, took his wife to the city of Ur, between Kufa and Basra, and hid her in a cave. And this is how Prophet Abraham escaped death — he opened his eyes for the first time in the cave. Migration, which was to define his whole life, began while Abraham was in his mother's womb.

After Abraham was granted the sacred duty of prophethood, he first conveyed the true religion to his father. Azar, who earned a living from sculpting and selling idols, naturally rejected his son's call to faith. Then by various means, for years Prophet Abraham preaches about God to his people, and tells them that their idols are worthless. The result is the same; the people reject Prophet Abraham's message.

One day, Prophet Abraham has an idea. During a festival, when the people had traveled to celebrate, Abraham enters the holy temple where all of the idols were kept. Except for the largest idol, the chief of all the manmade deities, he destroys every deity in the temple, smashing them to pieces. Then he placed his axe in the chief idol's arms. When they returned from the celebrations, the people were astonished, and began to speculate about the culprit. Knowing how he despised idols, the people were sure it must have been Prophet Abraham.

They called him and asked if he destroyed the idols. Prophet Abraham wanted to make them understand that they worshipped nothing but lifeless objects. He gave an ingenious answer and spoke about himself in the third person: "Rather, he must have done it." After a pause, he pointed at the axe on the largest idol's neck, "this is the biggest of them. Ask them, if they are able to speak!"

There was a murmuring throughout the crowd, and a shuffling of feet. A voice from the crowd cried:

"You know very well that our gods cannot talk!"

Abraham replied:

"Your gods cannot talk, but you worship them?"

Among a few of them, there was a feeling of unease bordering on regret. For a moment, they questioned their own beliefs, and thought: "Abraham is not the culprit, we are, for worshiping helpless, manmade gods." But in the tumult of the crowd, they ignored their consciences.

Abraham continued:

"You worship these helpless idols that cannot benefit you, but you refuse to worship the true God! Shame on you, and shame on those manmade statues you call gods! Why do you persist in your ignorance?"

In a fury, despite Abraham's words of warning, the crowd denied the unity of God. They decided to punish Prophet Abraham by casting him into a blazing fire. King Nimrod gave the order. An enormous heap of wood was stacked and set ablaze, and he was thrown into the ferocious flames.

But on the command of God Almighty:

"O fire! Be cool and peaceful for Abraham."

And the center of the flames turned into a garden. When the fire died down, the people are stunned to see Abraham sitting unharmed in the center of the smoldering wood. But still they would not believe.

Then the sacred migration of Prophet Abraham began. Realizing that his people would remain in arrogant disbelief, he traveled to various regions with his wife, Sarah, his nephew, Lot, and the few among his people who believed. After staying in Harran and Jordan for awhile, Prophet Abraham traveled to Egypt, and then settled in Palestine. Ibrahim then married Hajar, who gave birth to his firstborn son, Ishmael. After the birth of Ishmael, another migration awaited Prophet Abraham, which is why he traveled to Mecca.

Reflections

A statement which achieves the speaker's clear aim is an expression that portrays meaning within a paragraph, sentence or within the boundaries of a sentence. A verbal statement that does not portray one's true intention is known as an "expression beyond intent." In a sense, it means to falter. Statements that deliberately conceal the true meaning are known as word manipulation. When Prophet Abraham was asked who had destroyed the idols, he used a form of word manipulation that caused people to question their assumptions.

In a sacred mission, migration is a very important factor. Many great figures who fought for a cause had to migrate. Those who recognized the significance of a sacred mission abandoned their homelands for the sake of the cause, and traveled to foreign regions. Performing the migration for the sake of God deems it an abundant, rewarding action. One who migrates for the sake of God is certain to get positive results in his future endeavors. It is an important event in a believer's life.

The stages of the life of Prophet Abraham are full of lessons and warnings for today's Muslims.

THE LAST PERSON TO
ENTER PARADISE

Prophet Moses was a messenger who had the honor to speak with God, asked his Lord for information about certain matters, and then shared the answers with his community. One day this question came to his mind:

"I wonder what the Paradise for the lowest rank of the inhabitants will be like."

God the Almighty gave this reply:

"My servants who have been granted Paradise will be admitted one by one until there is only one of My servants left behind. He will be told: "Enter Paradise." And My servant will take a step to enter, but Paradise will appear full to him. Then this conversation will take place between Me and My servant:

"My Lord! All the people have settled in Paradise, but unfortunately there is no place left for me."

"My servant! Would you not be content to live a life of comfort like the kings of the world?"

"I have not been a righteous enough servant to deserve this, but Your favor and charity is plentiful. Yes, I would be content, my Lord!"

"I will grant you this and four times more."

"I am well pleased, my Lord! But I do not know what to say."

"In addition, I will grant you ten times more."

The Lord's answer pleased Moses immensely. Then he asked another question:

"O Lord! If this is the condition of those at the lowest level of Paradise, then what will those at the highest level of Paradise be granted?"

"I will grant them rewards that no eyes have ever seen, no ears have ever heard and which no human could ever imagine."

When Prophet Moses heard of the blessings to be granted by his Lord, he fell to his knees, proclaiming words of praise and gratitude.

Reflections

Every believer wishes to enter Paradise according to their rank. God describes the rewards that we could be granted in the afterlife in order to further stimulate this desire. Since humans are mainly under the influence of the physical world, this is presumably why God constantly describes heaven's material beauties. But there are blessings that exceed our imagination and perception — such as observing the beauty of God — which promises to be the most important of all blessings.

This world is a harvest field for the world beyond. The good deeds and worship of this world are rewarded in the Hereafter with blessings of a nature that we are unfamiliar with. Likewise, certain events which seem unfavorable in this world may have favorable results. For example, worship such as prayer, charity and hajj will come before us as blessings in Paradise; likewise, the difficulties, afflictions and illnesses endured in this world will come before us as blessings in Paradise.

The Prophet thus comforted Abu Hurayrah, who was performing his prayers in the sitting position and shedding tears due to hunger and weakness:

"O Abu Hurayrah! Do not weep, for those who suffer from hunger in this world will not sense the pangs of hunger in the Hereafter."

One's efforts to resist carnal desires and to become an honorable person, content with the lawful pleasures and indulgences of this world, avoiding what is prohibited, will appear as blessings in Paradise. The seeds of reward are sowed in this world, and its harvest will be reaped in the Hereafter. Our actions and deeds are selected, and like harvested wheat, pass through the grind mill of this world, and produce a harvest that is stored until the afterlife. Every soul that is created in this world is brought to life in the next. The good deeds are packaged in this world, and presented to us one by one in the world of eternity, which in turn is transformed into a life of wonder and prosperity.

As every blessing of this world reminds us of the Creator; everything in the Hereafter will also remind us of God the Almighty. God, the power of the heavens and the earth, Who describes Himself as the Compassionate and the Merciful. As a hadith of the Prophet relates, only a fraction of God's mercy is shown in this world. The remainder of His mercy will manifest in the Hereafter. Such an outpouring of mercy to humans will nearly transform the people of Paradise, so to speak, into angels.

THE MANSION OF PRAISE

Mahmud was an ethical, trustworthy young man who was well educated by his mother and father. The person he loved most in the world was his grandmother. She taught him a great deal on religious thought, and her advice about gratitude touched him the most:

"My dear grandson! We are weak and helpless, but our needs are great. Our Lord's mercy and favor is so vast, He has bestowed us with innumerable blessings. However much we praise and glorify God, it is not enough. Therefore, constantly glorify your Lord until your very last breath, whether you are favored with good things or afflicted with bad things. Always glorify and praise God for whatever He bestows upon you." Mahmud adhered to his grandmother's advice, and constantly praised his Lord.

When Mahmud had grown up and reached a suitable age for marriage, on the advice of his elders, he married a young girl who came from a good family. Like himself, she was devoted to her religion. Mahmud and his wife were extremely happy. They were careful not to offend each other, and lived peacefully and contentedly. But there was something missing in their happy home. Before long, the couple was given the good news: Mahmud was going to be a father. He was elated, and performed ablution and prostration of gratitude, and then supplicated to his Lord:

"O Lord! Although I am not worthy, You bestow me with eternal blessings. I fail to show gratitude as I should for Your favor and benefaction. Grant us with a child of purity, and never allow this child to stray from Your path."

The following nine months passed quickly. Mahmud's wife gave birth to a beautiful, healthy baby boy, and they agreed to name him Abdullah. With their son's birth, major changes came to their lives, for the couple had now become a true family. They rearranged their lives completely for their beloved son.

Three years passed, and Abdullah learned to speak. At home, he was mischievous and made his mother and father laugh. As his father prayed, Abdullah would stand beside him and pray, too. In the evenings, Mahmud would read aloud while Abdullah sat with his mother and listened.

Suddenly one night, amidst a life of bliss, Abdullah became ill with a dangerously high temperature. Naturally, his mother panicked, and Mahmud comforted his wife:

"He will be fine. He has had a high temperature before and nothing happened. Fetch some water and a towel and we will try to lower his temperature."

The couple tried to lower Abdullah's temperature all night long, but their efforts were in vain. Dark circles formed beneath their child's eyes. Mahmud rushed out of the house to call a doctor. Traveling to the doctor, who lived in the town, would take three hours. Mahmud traveled a total of six hours — three hours to town, and three hours to return to the village. The doctor went straight to Abdullah's room and examined him. The little boy was in a poor state. From the expression on the doctor's face, his mother realized that something was seriously wrong with her son.

"Doctor! Please tell me, he is going to get better, isn't he?"

Without replying, the doctor called Mahmud out of the room. He told Mahmud that it was too late, that his son would only live for a short time. Then the doctor returned to the town. When Mahmud went back into the room, his wife's eyes were bloodshot from crying. He knelt beside his son's bed and stroked his head. Deeply sad, he was unable to hold back his tears. As the tears rolled down Mahmud's cheeks, he spoke to Abdullah:

"My dear little son! Your life with us has been a short one, but if God wills we will be united again in Paradise. Our Lord sent you to us as a precious gift. He is the giver of both life and death. Accepting His command is our duty, all praise and glory to the Lord."

Then the baby took his last breath…

In the meantime, there was a conversation between God and Azrail, the angel of death:

"Did you take the soul of My servant's fruit of life, his dear son?"

"Yes, O Lord!"

"How did My servant react? What did he say?"

"O Lord! He displayed outstanding patience, and he praised You saying, 'Indeed, we belong to God, and to Him we shall return.'"

"Prepare a mansion for My servant in Paradise and call it 'the mansion of praise.'"

Reflections

Humans are sent to this world for a series of trials beginning in childhood, and lasting until the moment when the soul is resigned to the Lord. Without doubt, one of the greatest of these trials is the loss of a child. In a hadith, the Prophet states that a child who dies before reaching puberty will be a shield for his parents against the flames of Hell.[9]

We must realize the importance of praising everything that comes from God. He is the Giver and the Retriever. Accepting whatever God bestows upon us, and always responding to blessings and difficulties with gratitude and without complaint, is one of the basic principles of belief. Those who adhere to this principle gain the pleasure of their Lord.

In the original hadith this story is based on, the conversation which takes place between God and the angels following the death of a believer's child is mentioned.

---

[9]   Muslim, 1606.

WHERE ARE YOU TAKING ME?

Once upon a time, there were two men who had grown up together in the same neighborhood. When they were young, they were the best of friends. They played together and spent all of their free time together.

Many years passed. One of the men had followed in his father's footsteps and become a merchant, while the other had studied and become a scholar. Though the men still lived in the same neighborhood, their friendship was very different than before.

The merchant was the owner of many properties and substantial wealth, he was the richest man in the neighborhood. But his wealth had led him astray, and distracted him from his duties to God. Over a period of time, he had even begun to deny the existence of God. It grieved the scholar, his childhood friend, who prayed continuously that he would repent. The scholar visited the merchant on several occasions and tried to make him see sense, but his efforts were in vain.

"Leave all this nonsense, my dear friend! We only come into this world once, this is where we experience everything in life, and this is the end," the merchant said. "There is no life after this. Look, the only reason I am so polite is because we have been friends for so long, or believe me things would be different. You know that I have great respect for you. Please change the subject."

So the scholar went home, where he continued to increase his knowledge and servitude.

Many years passed, and the two friends were on their deathbeds. In a short time, each man took his final breath. They had passed from this illusory world to the world of truth. In the Hereafter, every human will be granted the reward or punishment for the life he lived in this world. Privileged are those who recognized this world as a world of trials, who acted with patience and gratitude, and in turn are rewarded with Paradise.

The scholar, as he was carried in his coffin toward the graveyard, saw that his grave was a garden from those of Paradise. He pleaded with those carrying his coffin:

"Hurry, please walk a little faster! Deliver me to my abode immediately!"

He longed to reach the beautiful place that had been prepared for him as soon as possible. However, none of those present could hear him…

A short time later, the merchant who rejected faith was likewise carried toward the graveyard in his coffin. In death, he recognized the truth of the life he had rejected. The merchant deeply regretted his actions, but it was too late. He cried out to those who were carrying his coffin:

"Oh no! Where am I going? Where are you taking me? You cannot put me into that dungeon of Hell. No! Please do not put me down there!"

None of those present could hear him either.

As the Prophet related in a hadith:

"His voice can be heard by everything except humans. If humans could hear these cries, they would lose their balance, and fall unconscious."

Reflections

A human is a traveler in this world. It is a journey that begins in the spiritual world, and travels into this world from the mother's womb, through childhood, youth, adulthood and old age, the journey continues from the grave on to either Paradise or Hell. But how aware are humans of this long journey?

If a person does not think of death and be prepared for it by leading a decent life and practicing worship, it would be impossible to avoid or escape from the traps of Satan.

But if a human considers himself to be a continuous traveler, he will remember death, and be conscious of his duties, and he will avoid the illusory adornments of this world that make the journey more difficult.

Those who refuse to see behind the material world become confined to the flesh and imprisoned by the bodily desires. In order to revive spirituality and remorse, a person must destroy the materialistic and the egoistic aspects of existence. This world and the Hereafter are two faces of one truth. Considering the two individually is irrational, and a believer must be moderate and balanced in his actions. In short, it is necessary to base this world on the next.

The world is a field of prosperity for the Hereafter, and a unique opportunity for humans to earn their abode in Paradise. There is a very close relationship between this world and the Hereafter. In the Qur'an, God the Almighty provides us with crucial boundaries regarding both: "But seek, by means of what God has granted you, the abode of the Hereafter, without forgetting your share in this world. Do good to others as God has done good to you. Do not seek corruption and mischief in the land, for God does not love those who cause corruption and make mischief" (Qasas 28:77).

The words "without forgetting your share in this world" indicate that a person should not abandon the world entirely, but must seek to live an honorable and valuable life.

The grave is like a garden of heaven to the righteous, and is like a dungeon of to the evil. The grave is a reflection of one's actions. A saying of the Prophet relates: "Prayer is a (blessed) light, and charity is a proof (of faith, and a means of spiritual guidance)."[10]

Prayer is light in the dark grave and charity is proof of sincere faith. They are shields that protect believers, like guards, in their graves from discomfort and anguish.

---

[10]   Nasai, Zakah; Muslim, Taharah, 1; Tirmidhi, Jumah 80.

Another hadith of the Prophet: "When the body is laid in the grave, even before the sound of the footsteps of his companions disappear, two angels come and question him. At that moment a source of light appears and sits beside him. This is his prayer. Another source of light comes and sits by his feet. This is his good deeds. Another source of light comes and settles on his right side. This is his fast. Then another source of light appears and settles on his left side, this is his charity. All these protect him from the narrowing walls, and from the punishment of the grave."[11]

The grave can be a treasure chest of good deeds. When we reach eternity, we will find our prayers, fasts, charity and good deeds protecting us there.

---

[11]   Abdurrazzak, Musannaf 3/582, 583.

THE EARLY BIRD

In ancient times, there lived a merchant by the name of Sakr. He traded in dried food products and became very wealthy in a short period of time. Sakr was a hardworking, trustworthy, well-respected merchant who never deceived his customers and always paid his workers on time. He traded in his own area and in neighboring regions.

Sakr's fellow traders wondered about the reason for his success and prosperity in business, but were hesitant to ask. One of them decided to visit him at his shop.

"I will go and ask Sakr the secret of becoming so rich in such a short time."

Sakr was pleasant and hospitable. Then the man asked:

"Please forgive my curiosity. I was wondering, well, to be truthful, all of the traders around here are curious about your success in business. How did you achieve such wealth so quickly?"

With a smile on his face, Sakr answered:

"For years, I have made a habit of opening my shop very early in the morning. I open the doors at dawn every morning without fail. I never go back to sleep after I have woken up. This is my habit, and I assume that this is why the Lord blessed me with success in my business, and granted me such prosperity."

The man was satisfied, and rushed off to share the secret with his fellow traders.

Reflections

Sleep is a divine blessing that relaxes our bodies and prepares us for the next day. Those who lack sleep from long working hours realize the value of the blessing even more. Scholars tell us which times are most suitable for sleep, and which times are undesirable for sleep. For example, in the time from dawn until sunrise — forty or fifty minutes after the break of dawn — it is not advisable to sleep. According to a hadith, this form of sleep causes a decrease and unproductiveness in provision, and is contrary to the practices of the Prophet. The time most appropriate for preparing to work for one's sustenance is when it is cool, the early hours of the day. When this time has passed, lethargy descends. It has been established through numerous experiences that not only is lethargy unfavorable for daily work and gaining one's livelihood but it also causes unproductiveness. When we spend this time asleep, we usually feel more tired. When we begin the day feeling tired, our duties throughout the day are affected. But those who have sufficient sleep and remain awake during the stated times will prosper and will be more tranquil in their daily activities. It is reported that the Prophet prayed for his community as follows: "O God, bless my people in their early mornings."

Scientists, too, advise arranging sleep according to the sun. Before dawn, the brain should be alert and prepared for the day ahead. According to scientists, sleeping after dawn makes a person feel more tired, not more relaxed. Sleeping during this time causes swelling and expanding of the brain, which imbalances the functions of the nervous system. Those who seek prosperity in their lives and work should abstain from sleeping after the morning prayer.

They say that the livelihood of the early riser prospers. It is a reflection of the Prophet's supplication for God to bless the livelihood of those who begin the working day early.

IMPORTANCE OF FORGIVENESS

Jafar was a merchant of textiles, known to all as a trustworthy, hardworking, self-sacrificing and generous man. He never forgot to distribute a portion of his earnings to the needy, especially to poor students. His generosity encouraged his fellow traders to be charitable, as well. Jafar was a fine example, loved and highly respected by those around him.

Jafar devoted his life to charity. As God had bestowed him with wealth, he bestowed charity to the poor. Jafar was also a forgiving man. He was gracious to his family, friends and employees. He never criticized people for making mistakes and kindly excused them, and thus won the hearts of everyone he knew.

Jafar grew very old and ill. On his deathbed, with his children and family around him, his last words were:

"My dear children, I am about to leave this world. Give me your blessings and renounce your rights. If I have rights over any of you, know that I renounced my rights to you all long ago. Always support each other and protect the poor. Never prolong any disputes you may have among yourselves. Always be forgiving and strive for peace."

A few hours later, Jafar took his last breath and passed away. Although God was well aware of His servant's actions in this world, He asked:

"My servant, I granted you with great wealth and possessions. What did you do for Me?"

"My Lord, You know that I was a person of forgiveness. I never refused a person in need. I forgave those who were unable to repay their debts."

Then God commanded His angels:

"Accept My servant into Paradise. I am more worthy of forgiving than My servant."

Reflections

Asking forgiveness is a virtue, but forgiving others is much a greater one, a sign of excellence. The common phrase "forgiveness is a virtue," though short, contains volumes of wisdom. Forgiveness is rectification, requiring a return to the soul and rediscovery. The struggle of pursuing forgiveness, against the blame and censure which bring the soul anguish, is one of the most loved actions in the eyes of God the Forgiving.

Just as one wants to be forgiven, so he must also forgive. Is it possible for a person who strives to escape the flames of meanness that burn deep in his soul, who eventually quenches his thirst in the river of forgiveness, not to excuse others? Especially if that person knows that the means of forgiveness is by forgiving others — because we know that those who forgive will be forgiven, but those who are not merciful to others, will not be shown mercy.

On occasion, when a person is not able to pay his debt due to the indigence, displaying patience and kindness is the duty of the creditor, who should not place any more difficulty on the debtor. The debtor, in turn, must pay the loan at the earliest possible time to escape the burden of debt.

The Qur'anic term *qard al-hasan*, "a goodly loan," is based on the Islamic ideal of giving interest-free loans to needy people solely for the pleasure of God. It is based on belief and kindness. Since only those who are in need ask for loans, and since loans universally involve interest, the debtor is always the only one who suffers in the long run.

(The name "Jafar" we used for the main character of the story is not mentioned in the hadith.)

THE MAN WHO SLEPT FOR A HUNDRED YEARS

Long ago, a young man lived in a tiny village. He was always deep in thought, because he loved to study the wonders of the universe. He travelled long distances away from the village and climbed up into the hills, where he observed the beauty of creation, and attempted to truly appreciate the greatness of the Lord. After dark, he stared up into the dark sky, observed the movement of the moon and the stars and said:

"O Lord! I wonder how many more planets there are up there, invisible to the human eye. As I observe Your power and might, I realize just how much of a helpless creature I really am. I am so astonished that humans can still deny Your existence after witnessing the excellence of Your creation."

One day, the young man set out with his donkey to observe the wonders of God's creation. He had travelled quite a long way, and reached a place where he had never been before. From a distance, the place appeared deserted. But as he ventured closer, the young man saw ruins. He realized the ruins had once been a village. Long before, all of the village's residents had died, and their homes had been destroyed. The ruins were all that remained.

Gradually it started to get dark. Searching for a place to spend the night, the young man thought, "I will stay here tonight, and return home at the first light of dawn." He noticed a cave nearby. He mounted his donkey, and decided to seek shelter there for the night. The young man tied his donkey to a tree next to the cave's entrance.

In the captivating darkness, the young man became lost in thought. The moonlight shone on the village ruins. At that moment — like Prophet Abraham, whose curiosity made him eager to see with his own eyes what his heart already knew —the young man thought:

"Could the Lord give life once again to this village of ruins, and make it just as it was in the old days?"

As the thought passed through his mind, the young man drifted off into a deep sleep. His slumber lasted for exactly one hundred years, and then he was awakened by the command of God. It was morning when he emerged from the cave that had been his shelter for a century. He could not believe his eyes. Before him was a village buzzing with activity, where people worked, animals roamed and children played. He was amazed and frightened. Extraordinary things were happening that were beyond his understanding.

A man approached him through the bushes in the distance. The young man assumed that he was a resident of the village. But then the man greeted him, sat beside him and explained that he was an angel sent by God, disguised as a mortal. The angel asked, "How long have you been here?"

The young man replied, "Since late last night."

"No, you have been in this cave for exactly a hundred years," the angel said. "God concealed you here as an example to the people. If you do not believe me, take a look at your donkey."

The young man had forgotten the donkey and began to look around for the poor animal. Then he remembered that he had tied it to a tree beside the cave's entrance. As he searched the area, he noticed sun-bleached animal bones in the exact place where he tied it up.

"See! Those are the bones of your donkey. Its bones have been lying there like this for years."

Suddenly, an extraordinary thing happened. Before the young man's eyes, flesh began to form around the donkey's bones. Quickly it took shape before him, and then came back to life. The donkey had been resurrected.

After witnessing this miracle, the young man said:

"O Lord, now I have a greater understanding, and I truly believe that You bear the power sufficient to incur whatever You will. Just as You created the universe from nothing, You will give us life again after death. You are the Creator and the owner of this universe. O Lord! You are free from imperfection. Your glory and eminence is so great!"

Reflections

Contemplation is a very important in the life of a Muslim. The Qur'an tells us: "Surely in the creation of the heavens and the earth, and the alternation of night and day, there are signs for the people of discernment." (Al-Imran 3:190)

Indeed, there is harmony in the rising and setting of the sun and moon, in the enduring, dazzling balance of the whole universe. As the Prophet said in a hadith: "Shame on he who reads this verse, and does not consider the wonders of God's creation." Umm Salamah, the dear wife of the Prophet, reported that he wept when he recited this verse of the Qur'an. The Qur'an is a light of guidance, which encourages readers to think and reflect.

The foundation of thought is reading and reflecting, as well as keeping the heart and mind open. As the Holy Qur'an encourages, we must observe the wonders of existence. Pondering the utterance of God, we will learn the principles of true faith. As we contemplate the earth's wonders, there will come a moment when we awaken to our own lives. All of existence will stand together, side by side, rather like a parade of respect before the Lord. In summertime, trees, flowers, and plants of all hues and sizes reach toward the sky and sun, aligned like uniformed soldiers before their Lord.

Then autumn arrives, and leaves fall, and creation is in a state of devastation. With the harsh, destructive winds of autumn, the surface has turned gray as if from scattered cinders. We tread as if we are walking through a deserted wilderness. And then winter sets in. Snow covers the ground and there is no sign of life. Plants wither and perish, and trees become skeletal. Life has come to an end.

Then, in the spring, something flourishes in the remains of the devastation. We look around, and the gloomy, dried trees become adorned again, standing upright before their Lord. The withered, shriveled foliage disappears as flowers, leaves and seeds find the strength to grow, and burst back to life. Insects open their eyes from the winter slumber, sensing the purified air that they will breathe blowing gently on their bodies, finding a plentiful supply of greenery growing in the soil. The Lord gathers and gives life to millions of insects every spring.

Observing the seasons every year, we reach the conclusion that after death, we too will be gathered and given new life just like this. The Qur'an indicates this:

> "Say: Go about on the earth and see how God originated creation. Then God will bring forth the other creation. Surely God has full power over everything." (Al-Ankabut 29:20)

> "Look, then, at the imprints of God's Mercy – how He revives the dead earth after its death: certainly then it is He Who will revive the dead (in a similar way). He has full power over everything." (Ar-Rum 30:50)

If the One who commands the creation of millions of creatures and life annually without confusion, also promises to give us life again after He takes it away, how could this be beyond His power? Can we disbelieve a craftsman who invents a machine from nothing, removes all the pieces and dismantles his invention, and then claims to have the ability to restore the machine to its original state? If a commander who creates an army from nothing and trains the soldiers under his regulations, claims to have the power to gather the dispersed soldiers at the sound of a horn, who can argue?

Even these lowly examples are sufficient to convince anyone of reflection that it is impossible to deny the afterlife. Thought plays a large part in gaining our Creator's affection. One hour of contemplation can sometimes induce depth in the faith of a believer, depth that may never be achieved even through long periods of worship.

THE FOUR DEAD BIRDS

One day, Prophet Abraham noticed the carcass of an animal on the seashore. He observed it for awhile. As the waves flowed in with the tide, fish nibbled at the carcass; when the sea ebbed and receded, wild animals feasted on the remains. Birds of prey perched above the carcass, full from their earlier feast. After they had picked the carcass clean, the animals disappeared. The flesh of a single dead animal had satisfied the hunger of many others.

This, too, is the case with humans. When a human is buried beneath the soil, the body decomposes and becomes part of the earth. When humans die above ground, they are eaten by insects or wild animals, and those who drown are eaten by fish. A dead body does not remain intact, but decomposes.

God will give life to the dead; decayed flesh and bones will be resurrected — but how? Prophet Abraham wanted to understand in this world and asked his Lord:

"O Lord! Show me how You give life to the dead."

God replied:

"O Abraham! Do you not believe (that I can give life to the dead)?"

"Yes, but that my heart may be at rest."

God ordered Abraham to take four birds, familiarize himself with those birds, and then slaughter them, cut their flesh into pieces and then place a portion of their flesh on four separate hills and call them. God told him that the birds would come to him flying.

Prophet Abraham found a peacock, a chicken, a falcon and a crow to fulfill his Lord's command. He fed and tended to the birds until he was familiar with each of them. Abraham wanted to be able to recognize the birds when they flew back to him. After awhile, the birds trusted Prophet Abraham, and he was able to distinguish between his birds and others. Finally, one day Prophet Abraham did as God commanded. He slaughtered the four birds, placed a portion of flesh on four hills, and returned home. Then he called the birds.

The flesh of each of the four birds miraculously became whole and alive, and the birds flew back to Prophet Abraham; he prostrated in praise and glorified his Lord. He believed deep in his soul that God, the One who rejoined the flesh of the dead birds and gave them life, undoubtedly possessed the power to recreate and reanimate the bodies of humans buried beneath the soil.

Reflections

It is natural for people to want to see with their own eyes what they believe and affirm in their souls. This was why Prophet Abraham wanted to witness God giving life to the dead. Prophet Abraham had faith in God's power and ability, but he was curious how resurrection occurred. In addition, this case presents an example for those to come after him and strengthens their belief on bodily resurrection.

Although God knew His prophet's motive, the question "do you not believe?" is intriguing. By asking, God had provided Abraham with the opportunity of verbally expressing his intention, preventing future generations who heard the story from misunderstanding Prophet Abraham's intentions.

God forbid someone should claim that the Creator, who created humans from nothing, is "incapable" of recreating the bodily structure after death. Undoubtedly God has the power to give life again, just as, every spring, He resuscitates the roots that died during winter. We know that on the Day of Judgment, God will resurrect those who have decayed in their graves.

Our Lord has granted us, His servants, with benevolence we are hardly even aware of. It is our duty to consider the innumerous blessings God bestowed upon us, and to glorify and praise the Lord throughout our lives for the blessings that we take for granted.

THE LOST CAMEL

A man had to leave immediately, for there was a long, tiring and difficult journey through the desert ahead of him. Loading water and supplies onto his camel, he set out on his journey.

It was noon, and as the penetrating heat of the sun reached its peak, he had completed just half of his journey. He noticed a few trees in the distance and thought:

"I have been travelling since the break of dawn. Both me and the camel are very tired. First we will rest under these trees until it gets a bit cooler, then we will continue the rest of the journey."

He tied his camel to a tree, and rested under its shade. A few hours passed. When the man woke up, he began to look around frantically — his camel had disappeared. It was quite likely that, in his fatigue, he had not tied the rope tightly enough. Everything he needed to live was on his camel: water, food, a blanket, a gun. Most importantly, completing the journey without the camel was impossible.

What would he do? He began to search for his camel. The poor man looked everywhere, but the camel was nowhere to be found. It was as if it had disappeared into thin air. He had no choice; either he found the camel, or faced death. He was alone in the desert. He may be able to live without certain things, but how long could he live without water?

Without wasting another minute, he set off in search of his camel. He traveled for quite a distance, but there was still no sign of the animal. Then the sun began to set on the horizon, so he decided to find a place to rest for the night, and continue his search early the next morning.

The man was desperate. Raising his hands toward the heavens, he supplicated:

"O Lord! I am here alone in this vast desert, abandoned to my fate. O Lord, help me! Please do not abandon me to die in this isolated desert."

Exhausted, the man slept deeply. When he awakened, he could not believe his eyes. The camel that he had spent the afternoon searching for was standing right beside him. At first he thought it was a dream, but then he heard the camel chewing. The man stood and hugged the camel around its curved neck. He searched the saddlebag, and found the water, food and all his belongings were still there. He was so overwhelmed with joy that he raised his hands toward the heavens, and instead of saying "O Lord! All praise be to You, You are my Lord, and I am Your servant," he said:

"O Lord! I am Your Lord and You are my servant."

After relating this story, the Prophet said: "God is more pleased with the repentance of his servant, than the man who found his lost camel in the desert."

Reflections

Repentance is reform, an inner amendment against sin. By repenting, we seek refuge from the punishment of God and in His blessing, we seek mercy and grace from His reckoning. We all come into this world innocent and free of sin. When we reach the age of responsibility, the choice of two paths appears before us. One will lead us to the dungeons of Hell, the other to Paradise. On occasion, we may stray from the path leading to Paradise. If we stray from the path of truth, we must say to ourselves: "Turn to your Lord in penitence and submit to Him wholly before the punishment comes upon you." (Az-Zumar 39:54) and return to the true path, indeed this will please the Lord immensely.

By repenting, we purify hearts stained by sin. This is mention by the Prophet in a hadith: "When the believer sins, a black spot forms on his heart. If he does not purify this with repentance, that black spot will remain on his heart. If he commits a second sin, another black spot will appear on his heart."[12]

Without wasting any time, a believer should purify his sins with repentance. Naturally, there is the continuous threat of straying from the true path again. We must motivate our minds and bodies, and try to strengthen the relationship between ourselves and our Creator by saying: "I have reached this position because I severed my ties with God. Therefore, my only means of salvation is by restoring my relationship with Him."

---

[12] Ibn Majah, Zuhd, 29.

YOU DID NOT VISIT ME

At the end of time, when life on earth has ended, people will stand before their Lord waiting to be questioned for their actions. At that moment, a conversation will take place between God and His servants:

"My servant! I fell ill but you did not visit Me."

"O Lord, how could I visit You! You are the Lord of the universe, how can you fall ill?"

"My servant! Did you not know that one of My servants was ill, but you did not visit him? Did you not know that if you had visited him, you would have found My pleasure with him?"

"My servant! I asked you for food, but you did not feed Me."

"O Lord! How could I feed You? You are the Lord of the universe. You are free from hunger, You do not need to eat or drink."

"One of My servants was hungry. He asked you for food but you did not feed him. Did you not know that if you fed him, you would have earned My affection, My approval and pleasure?"

"My servant! I asked you for water, but you did not give Me any."

"O Lord! How could I give You water? You are the Lord of the universe! You do not need water."

"My servant! One of My servants asked you for water, but you did not give him water. Did you not know that if you had given him water, you would have earned My approval and pleasure?"

Reflections

God has no needs; He never falls ill, feels hunger or thirst. One of His names is As-Samad, the Eternally Besought — all of existence depends on Him, but He is dependent on nothing.

However, God loves those who visit the sick, feeds those who are hungry, and gives water to those who are thirsty. Those who perform these good deeds, experience the joy and peace of earning the pleasure of God.

Visiting those close to us, not only when they are healthy, but also when they are ill, is a requirement. By witnessing the suffering of those who are sick, we realize how grateful we should be for health.

The Prophet, who said that visiting the sick was one of the five rights of a Muslim over another Muslim, encouraged all believers to visit the ill.[13] In which case, to please God, His Prophet and our Muslim brothers and sisters, we should never neglect visiting the sick.

---

13 Tirmidhi, Adab, 1; Bukhari, Janaiz 2.

THE ANGEL IN DISGUISE

Akif and Ali were very close friends with great affection for each other. Those around them envied the relationship of the devoted companions. The friends believed that doing charitable deeds was an effective way of amending errors. When a person is called to do good deeds by a person of goodwill, it reminds him of truth, and prevents him from straying from the path of righteousness.

One day, Akif wrote a moral contract. He called it "the agreement of goodwill" and it was meant to invoke kindness, inform friends of faults and help to rectify mistakes.

"I want us both to sign an agreement," Akif said.

"What kind of an agreement?" Ali asked.

"I am permitting you to inform me of my mistakes, or anything I do personally that you think is wrong."

"Okay, but I can only accept this on one condition. You must inform me of my mistakes, too."

"Okay, I agree."

The friends signed the contract, and became a "spirit of goodwill" to each other.

Many years passed, and their relationship was still as strong as ever. Then, because of work, Akif had to move to a different city, which grieved them both. The companions comforted one another, and promised to visit frequently. Theirs was a friendship for life.

After a month had passed, Ali missed his friend very much. Whenever Ali mentioned his name in conversation, his eyes would fill with tears. He could not wait any longer to see his dear friend, so he decided to visit.

On the way, he noticed a strange man. The man was sitting on the roadside, and looked as if he was trying to say something to him. Ali walked over to the man and greeted him. The man asked:

"Where are you off to, young man?"

"I am going to visit my friend," Ali replied.

"Your friend must have done you a great favor, and now you are going to thank him."

"No, I have nothing to thank him for. I love him for the sake of God and I am visiting him for the sake of God."

"How nice. I am going to tell you a secret. Now listen to me carefully. I am an angel sent to you by God. Know that just as you love your friend for the sake of God, God also loves you dearly."

Reflections

A human needs loyal friends just as much as he needs other things. An individual who finds peace and assurance with friends gains security and confidence in his own life. Loyalty to friends means experiencing their grief as if it is our own, and experiencing their joy as if it is our own. Those who feel no sadness in a friend's grief, and no pleasure in a friend's joy, are not loyal friends.

An intelligent person is one who quickly resolves problems in their relationships, and knows how to restore a friendship. An even more intelligent person is the one who never falls into bitter disagreement with friends.

The continuation of the love and trust between friends depends on the mutual consideration of understanding and self-sacrifice. Friends who have no mutual signs of altruism in their relationship, in thought or action, will never last. God loves those who are devoted and generous for one another, for His sake.

In a hadith, the Prophet gave those who attained the wisdom of brotherhood tidings from God: "Where are those who loved each other for the sake of My glory? On a day when there is no shade (the Day of Judgment), I will shade them with My own shade."

In the story, we used the names Akif and Ali rather than 'two men' as stated in the original hadith.

THE BORROWED PENDANT

Grandpa Ali was a man devoted to worship, and for his entire life, had been an example to those around him. He lived with his wife in a pleasant little town. The two elderly citizens had devoted their lives to their children, and provided them with a good education. One of their children became a doctor, one an imam and the other a teacher, and each of them had moved away to different parts of the country.

Each of the children wanted their parents to go and live with them, but Grandpa Ali and Granny Aisha refused to leave the town that had been their home for years. Living distant from their children had formed a closer bond between them.

On occasion, Grandpa Ali said:

"What will I do if you die before I do?" and his eyes filled with tears.

Granny Aisha, too, wept and replied:

"What will happen to me if you die first?"

Then Granny Aisha became ill, and Grandpa Ali took his wife to the doctor. She was diagnosed with cancer, and the doctor said she had a short time to live. The doctor's words devastated Grandpa Ali. As he took his wife home from the hospital, Granny Aisha gazed into her husband's eyes and said:

"I will be leaving you soon, my dear. With all our ups and downs, you have given me a good life, may the Lord be pleased with you. Will you forgive me for any mistakes I have made?"

Touched by his wife's words, Grandpa Ali replied:

"What have you ever done wrong? You should be forgiving me, you have put up with me for all these years."

A few days passed, and Granny Aisha became weaker. She was reaching the end of her time in this world. As Grandpa Ali was holding his dear wife's hand tightly, suddenly Granny Aisha's soul was taken by the angel of death.

Tears rolled down Grandpa Ali's cheeks, dampening his white beard. Their children came home for the funeral, and each of them tried to comfort their father.

After the death of his wife, Grandpa Ali went to live with his granddaughter, Nur, a student. Nur continued her studies, and also looked after her grandfather. Together, they frequently visited his wife's grave. But each visit there seemed to increase the old man's sorrow.

After her death, Grandpa Ali became grief-stricken. He pined for his wife deeply, and no one was able to comfort or reassure him — not his friends, not his relatives, not even his own children and grandchildren.

One day Nur prepared the evening meal, and called her grandfather to the table. As they sat together, Nur asked:

"Grandfather, I borrowed a pendant from one of my friends. I wore it for a while, and I really liked it. Now my friend wants me to return the pendant. Do you think I should give it back to her?"

"Of course you should return it, my dear. What kind of a question is that? You only borrowed it; you must return the pendant to its rightful owner."

"I know, but I have had it for so long now. I have gotten so attached to it, and I love it so much that, though I know deep down in my heart that it is hers, I want to keep it. Is there any way I may keep it?"

"My dear, this is even more reason to return the pendant. If you borrowed it from your friend ages ago, it is too late! Make sure you return it to your friend first thing tomorrow morning."

"Grandfather, listen to me carefully. Was my grandmother not an entrustment granted to you by God? You have been upset because He gave her to you for a time, and then took her away. But is He not the true owner?"

Grandpa Ali sat for a long time without saying a word, deeply considering his actions. He was guided to the truth by his granddaughter. He asked forgiveness from the Lord, and turned to Him in submission. For the rest of his life, Grandpa Ali glorified the Lord, and hoped to be reunited with his dear wife in the Hereafter.

Reflections

During youth, death may appear distant. A person may not realize that death comes to the young as well as the old. But as a person grows old, white hair, illness, and the passing of those around us are reminders of death. When an old person dies without faith, he is like a criminal sentenced to hanging. As the convict stands, trembling from fear, he waits for the order to step forward to the footstall, to be hung. The anticipation makes his life bitter and unbearable.

It is different for a person of faith. Faith comes to the rescue in the Hereafter, and the lives of old men changes with the tidings: "Do not fear! You have been granted eternal youth. An eternal life of prosperity awaits you. You will be reunited with your partners, friends and loved ones you lost, in happiness and bliss. As your good deeds have been recorded and protected, you will receive the reward." With such promises, even growing old a hundred times over would cause no distress.

We all have people close to us whom we love dearly. But we should not love people for the sake of their individual traits, but for the sake of God, the One who created the characteristics and the affection. When God takes the life of a loved one, we must try to redirect our sadness, and continue life with the hope that one day we will be reunited.

The characters in the hadith related to this story were originally unnamed.

THE MURDERER OF A
HUNDRED PEOPLE

J ust after the time of Jesus, there lived a dangerous murderer who was responsible for killing ninety-nine people. Over time he became aware of his guilt, and decided to repent for his sins. But would God accept the repentance of a man who had killed so many people? It was a question that constantly played on his mind. He thought:

"I must get advice from someone with knowledge, or I will never be at peace."

He asked those around him if they knew anyone who could help. They told him of a religious man who was considered learned. But he was a man of little knowledge, who had earned the trust of his community because of his servitude.

When he found the man, the murderer asked:

"I have killed ninety-nine people, but I deeply regret what I have done. I want to repent for my actions. If I ask His forgiveness, will God forgive me?"

Because the religious man had only basic knowledge, he was ill-equipped to answer. Yet he replied:

"It is far too late. God would never forgive a person who has killed so many people. He will never accept you repentance."

The man's reply vexed the murderer. As a wave of uncontrollable anger swept over him, he killed this man, too. He had murdered one hundred people.

Several days passed, and deep regret weighed on his heart. His shame became oppressive, and it led the murderer to search for another person who could help him. He asked everyone he knew:

"Do you know a man learned in religion who could advise me?"

This time, he learned of a truly qualified person, a scholar of religion. This man was an expert in religious topics, an intelligent and pious man, whose knowledge was reflected in every aspect of his life.

The murderer set out on the journey immediately, and went straight to the scholar's house. The scholar was very hospitable to his guest. After a short greeting, the murderer put the same question to the scholar. The scholar sensed the man's deep regret, and answered with the words:

"My dear son! The Lord is so compassionate. He accepts the repentance of all His servants. Even if you had committed a greater sin, He would still have forgiven you. But you must repent with sincerity and never commit the same sin again."

A smile appeared on the murderer's face, and a sense of relief washed over him. The scholar then explained the requirements of atonement:

"After asking God's forgiveness, you must leave your home and abandon the environment that you are living in, as this place is inviting you to sin. If you remain under the influence of these people, it is quite possible that you may commit the same sin again. Initially, you must deprive Satan of such an opportunity. So I will advise you of where you should go. Go and settle there. The people in that region are devoted to their worship, and they are a community of morality and wisdom. Establish a relationship with these people, but never go anywhere that will encourage you to sin, and never befriend people who may change you back to how you were before."

The man promised the scholar to do exactly as he said, and thanked him sincerely for his advice. He prayed to his Lord for forgiveness, then gathered all his possessions and departed for the community of believers. His repentance made him content, deep within his soul.

He had completed half of his journey, when the angel of death came to him. One never knows the specific time or place of one's death; it comes when we least expect it. The man took his last breath. The angels of mercy and punishment descended to earth to take him away.

The angels of mercy said:

"This man repented for his sins, so we are taking him."

The angels of punishment replied:

"No, we must take him. He may have repented to God for his sins, but he had no good deeds. He has not fulfilled the requirements of atonement."

The angels disputed among themselves about which should take the man's soul. As the argument continued, God sent another angel to judge between the two groups. The mediating angel said:

"Measure the distance between the city he left behind, and the city he was destined for. Whichever city he died closer to, that is where he belongs. If he died closer to the city where he committed sin, the angels of punishment shall take him; if he died closer to the city of believers, then the angels of mercy shall take him.

The angels measured the distance between the two cities, and it became clear that the man had died one step closer to the city of believers. The angels of mercy took him away.

Reflections

Repentance is inner amendment and reform. It is the individual seeking refuge in God from His punishment to ask for His favor, to cleanse the heart blackened by evil thoughts and behavior. Whatever the magnitude of the sin, the mercy of God is greater. If one sincerely regrets a sin, and turns to God asking to be forgiven, it is sufficient to gain forgiveness.

It is impossible for a person to avoid sin completely, because unlike angels, the souls of men are disobedient. A human being is prone to sinning and making mistakes. But more important is one's ability to recover after stumbling and to continue with more caution in the future. Sincere atonement and humility is what exalts humans to the level of angels.

The world of today has been transformed into an ocean of sin. Today, Satan and his accomplices stalk the face of the earth, waiting for men to sin on every corner. But believers must understand that in every sin, there is a path that leads to disbelief. A believer must turn toward the Creator with his mind and soul, and guard against sin.

Even if he catches only a glimpse or hears something accidently, a believer should take refuge in the Lord and express his regret: "O Lord! I have no idea how I did this, I stand before You in utter shame for committing this sin." The sorrow that surfaces from a believer's remorse should be so great that it embraces his entire being and puts the soul in harmony. A person who sincerely wishes to avoid sin after repenting, must also avoid the people and environment that support sinfulness. If regret is not expressed fully, or if the environment is not changed, the path to sin continues to be exposed, and Satan may again entice the believer down the path toward disbelief.

In a hadith, the Prophet said, "Man is influenced by the faith of his friends. Therefore, be careful of whom you associate with." The influence of society plays a large role in the faith of a Muslim. If our close friends and fam-

ily encourage us to live a righteous life, we are uncon-
sciously protected from the vicious cycle of sin and evil.
By virtue of such an environment, we live our lives on
the path of God with greater contentment. But if a person spends his life with those who delight in mischief and
sin, he will stumble and suffer a life of misery. We are
commanded in the Qur'an: "…and keep the company of
the truthful." (Tawbah 9:119)

THE TRIAL OF THREE PEOPLE

Long ago, there lived three men. One had a skin disease that covered his entire body, the second had lost all of his hair, and the third was blind. People constantly avoided contact with them, which grieved them.

God sent an angel to the man with the skin disease, who was squatting near a garbage dump, searching for food, and appeared to be very sad. Insects were buzzing around his head, but he ignored them. The angel approached him and asked:

"Would you like to be cured of this disease and regain the respect of the people?"

"Could you really cure me?"

"I am an angel sent to you by the mercy of God, and by the will of God I can cure you."

"In that case, I desperately want to be cured of this illness that makes people avoid me in the street, I would love to have beautiful, clear skin as soft as velvet."

The angel touched the man's flesh, saying "in the name of God." Instantly, he was cured of the disease, and began to dance with joy. When the angel saw his excitement, he asked:

"Would you like to be granted wealth sufficient enough that you will not be dependent on others?"

The man was elated and said: "Yes, I certainly would!"

"Which animal would you like?"

"I would like a camel, because camels are the most valuable animals in the region."

So the angel awarded him a camel that was about to give birth and said, "take this, may it be the means of your kindness."

Then the angel visited the bald man, who was sitting beneath a tree, sobbing. The angel approached him and asked:

"Would you like me to cure your baldness?"

"Well that sounds wonderful, but are you really capable of doing it?"

"I am an angel appointed by God, I was sent to cure you."

"Well, I would love to have thick, beautiful hair."

As soon as the angel touched the man's head, lustrous, beautiful black hair appeared on his head. He began to dance around in excitement. Then, just as he had with the previous man, the angel asked him which animal he wanted. When the man said "cattle," he was granted a cow instantly.

Last of all, the angel went to visit the blind man. He was struggling to find his way around with a crooked walking stick, sometimes walking into trees, tripping over stones or losing his balance and falling to the ground.

There was nobody around to help him. The angel approached him, and said that he could cure him just as he had cured the others. Then, in the name of God, the angel touched the man's eyes. The first words uttered by the blind man after his sight was restored were: "Eternal praise and glory to the Lord!"

The angel asked him what else he wanted. The man replied:

"You restored my sight, and I am very grateful. This is more than enough."

"But you must ask for something, it is the command of God."

"Well, if it really necessary, then I just want one sheep. That is more than enough."

So the angel granted the man his wish, and departed reciting words of supplication.

Many years passed. The man who had been cured of the skin disease owned a valley full of camels, so many that even he had lost count. The formerly bald man owned pastures full of cattle, and grew wealthier with every passing day. The man who had been blind was also one of the richest men in the region, living on the proceeds of sheep's milk and wool.

But a trial awaited the three men who had been granted health and abundance.

The man who had suffered the skin disease sat in his tent eating a lavish meal, proudly surveying his valley of camels. The sound of their groans mingled with songs sung by the shepherds, and echoed throughout the entire valley. Suddenly an angel, disguised as a man whose skin was blistered and flaky, approached the tent. Indeed, he looked like the camel owner from years past. The angel walked up to him and said:

"I am a very poor man, I have lost everything I owned. Now I want to return to my homeland, but I need your help. In the name of the One who blessed you with such wealth and comfort, if you give me one of your camels I will be able to travel home, and I will pray for your health and prosperity."

The man frowned with anger and replied:

"Get out! I already give more than enough charity. I provide the needs of plenty like you."

But the angel did not budge. "You seem familiar," he said, looking into his eyes. "Are you the man who begged in the street, whose skin was covered in scores long ago due to a skin disease, and the entire community avoided you because of your ugly appearance? Are you the man pitied by God, who He cured and granted wealth?"

"No, you must be mistaken. This wealth was left to me by my father and grandfather."

The angel warned: "If you are lying, God will turn you back into who you were before." Then he left, and continued on his journey.

The man who was once bald sat wearing his best clothes in a tent erected in the middle of a pasture, looking proudly at his herds of cattle. Disguised as a poor man, the angel approached him:

"I am a very poor man, and the community refused to help me. I have not eaten for days, and I am very weak from hunger. In the name of God, the One who granted you such wealth and abundance, please help me."

But this man was even more abrupt and abusive than the man before, and refused to help him. The angel said:

"I recognize you. Are not you the man who lost all his hair, the man who God pitied and cured and then granted all this wealth?"

"No, of course not. I was born with this thick head of hair, and all my wealth was bequeathed to me by my father."

The angel warned: "If you are lying, God will turn you back into who you were before." Then he left, and continued on his journey.

Finally, the angel visited the third man whose sight had been restored. He was sitting beneath a tree, observing his sheep. The man was alone, with no lavish surroundings, no assistant or shepherd to help him. He cared for and sheared his sheep by himself. The angel, again disguised as a poor traveler, approached:

"I am a poor wayfarer. I have been travelling for days, and not found shelter or food to eat. In the name of God, the One who blessed you with your sight and all this wealth, if you give me one of your sheep to relieve my burden, I will pray to God for your health and prosperity."

"Yes, of course. I was blind, but God granted me vision and blessed me with all this wealth and abundance. You asked me for a sheep, but take as many as you wish, and leave me as many as you see fit. You ask for the sake of God, and I give for the sake of God, because He is the One who granted me this wealth."

The angel replied:

"May the Lord bless you, and your wealth. Including you, God subjected three men to a trial, a test to determine their sincerity. The other two became absorbed in wealth and conceit and had forgotten their beginnings."

After the camel owner's abrupt response to the angel, a contagious disease spread throughout his herds of camels, and every single camel perished. The man, too, fell ill with skin disease.

The fate of the cattle owner was no different. The sky was overcome with darkness, and dark clouds covered the pasture. Thunder rumbled and lightning struck the fields. Heavy rainfall began, and a deluge swept away everything in its path. Every head of cattle drowned in the flood. He shook with fury, and one by one, the hair on his head fell to the ground. Not long after, he was seen begging for food.

Reflections

The Lord has granted us various blessings, and it is our duty to share them with those less fortunate. Muslims believe that if they give in this world, they will reap the benefits in the Hereafter; donating from their wealth, for the sake of God, gives them pleasure. Whatever a believer donates is given from the heart, with the joy of worship. When he gives, he gives in secret to protect the receiver from feeling degraded or dishonored. Secret giving is the most blessed form of charity.

From the wealth God has entrusted to believers, believers must give charity. God is the true owner of wealth, and it should be distributed for His sake. Just as an employee has no right to boast about fulfilling the duties for which he is paid, a believer has no right to boast about fulfilling the duties for which God grants him paradise. A believer constantly praises the Lord for helping him succeed in his obligations. Those who do not remember the Lord will be deprived of His blessings. God distributes wealth in accordance with His pleasure, and expects for those with enough to be generous and share with those who do not. God does not grant wealth so the rich can hoard it and satisfy all their own desires. Rather, in accordance with God's pleasure, we must avoid greed and give to the needy, in the hopes that we may all remember God.

If those who avoid wastefulness and give generously are accepted into paradise, and if those who are greedy and selfish are swallowed by the flames of Hell, then a person must balance his life in this world with the Hereafter. The Qur'an states: "But seek by means of what God has granted you, the abode of the Hereafter without forgetting your share in this world. Do good to others as

God has done to you. Do not seek corruption and mischief in the land, for God does not love those who cause corruption and make mischief" (Al-Qasas 28:77). It is warning us to forget neither this world, nor the Hereafter. Do not ignore this world in seeking the bliss of heaven, and do not ignore heaven in seeking after this world's pleasures.

Imam Ali said, "There are many who worship God to gain His favors, but only a few who obey Him due to gratitude of these favors." These words briefly but excellently illustrate this story's lessons.

TRUE FRIENDS

Conversation is mutual communication and the sharing of experiences. Souls unite and experience similar emotions based on a mutual affinity or cause. In such a union, the concept of "all for one" prevails, and they can perceive spiritual unity. People find relief from affliction or an outlet for joy, and increase their knowledge and wisdom.

Ahmet and his friends gathered one day every week in order to talk, share problems, and remember God. One evening, Ahmet and his friends socialized and spoke about general issues. Amidst them was a newcomer, who had joined the gathering that evening for the first time. But he had not come with the intention of listening to the others, he came because he didn't want to reject his friends' persistent invitations any longer.

"I'll hang out here for tonight and have a decent meal, and never come again," he thought.

As the meeting continued, a group of angels descended from the heavens to visit the house. Their duty was to visit gatherings held in remembrance of God to inform God of those present at the gatherings. The angels listened to those present, then ascended to the heavens and reported:

"O Lord! We have come from Your devoted servant, Ahmet, and his friends. They praised and glorified You this evening, increased their faith, and now they request Your favor."

"Have they seen Me and they are praising Me in such a manner?"

"No, they have not seen You, O Lord!"

"What would they have done if they had seen Me?"

"If they had seen You, O Lord, they would worship and glorify You even more intensely."

"What did they ask for?"

"They asked for Your Paradise."

"Have they seen Paradise?"

"No, they have not seen it, O Lord!"

"If they saw it what would they have done?"

"If they saw Paradise, O Lord, they would have wish for it even more, and would make an even greater effort to earn it."

"What do they fear the most?"

"They fear the fires of Hell, O Lord!"

"Have they seen Hell?"

"No, they have not seen Hell, O Lord!"

"And what would they have done if they had seen Hell?"

"O Lord, they would be even more afraid, and they would be even more heedful of their actions."

"You are My witnesses, I forgive them all. They will be granted Paradise, and kept distant from Hellfire."

Then one of the angels said:

"O Lord, there was one among them who did not come to the gathering to glorify You, or to listen to the others glorifying You, he came for another reason."

On hearing this, the Lord replied:

"I have forgiven him, too. This is a gathering of such excellence that none of those amongst them can be inhabitants of hell. I forgive him by virtue of the others."

Reflections

As believers, these gatherings are as important as food and water, especially during an age when Satan and his accomplices use every possible means to deter humans from the true path. We need to share our feelings and problems; solidarity among believers helps them to be strong, and less tempted by Satan's whispers. A Muslim needs spiritual education, communication, socialization and confidence to breathe, or he will drown amidst the traps and plots organized by Satan. Attending frequent gatherings is an armor in the heedless world. We must not forget that God forgives those who gather to mention His name, and even forgives those among them with different intentions.

Abu'l Lais Samarkandi, one of the great men of wisdom said: "If a person sits with a learned man and has benefited from his knowledge, he gains seven assets. If he actually learns knowledge, then his reward is much greater. One, he will earn the excellence of one who wishes to gain knowledge. Two, he will be protected from the enticement of his ego throughout the gathering. Three, he will acquire his share when the Mercy of God ascends upon the gathering. Four, divine mercy ascends from the moment he leaves home to attend the gathering. Five, a reward for the act of obedience will be recorded for listening at the gathering. Six, if he listens but does not understand, and then affliction emerges in his heart, he will be granted forgiveness. Seven, he would have gained the hospitality of the people, and his heart will be more inclined toward and fonder of knowledge.

The character in the original hadith was not referred to by name.

THE HURRICANE

I n ancient times, the tribe of Ad lived in what is now Yemen, north of the city of Hadramawt. The people of Ad lived in Ahqaf, which meant "sand dunes," and they constructed tall, sturdy buildings on the mountains, and were a very wealthy community. The people had a tall, broad stature, and were proud and boastful enough to claim: "there is no stronger nation in the entire universe."

The Creator sent Prophet Hud to the people of Ad, who had strayed from the path of God, and had begun to worship idols. Hud told his people they were on the wrong path. Not only did they ignore his warnings, they abused him. One day, he went to a place where the people gathered and said:

"O, my people, worship God alone; there is no deity other than Him. Will you not avoid disobedience to Him and strive to earn His protection?"

One of the people called out:

"You are foolish and weak-minded, and we are sure that you are a liar."

Distraught and saddened by their remarks, Prophet Hud replied:

"O, my people! There is no folly and weak-mindedness in me, rather I am messenger of the Lord of the worlds. I convey to you the messages of my Lord. I am a trustworthy counselor to you. Do you think it is strange that a reminder from your Lord should come from a man from among you? Remember and be mindful that He made you the successors of Noah's people, and increased you in stature and power. Remember and be mindful of God's bounties, that you may prosper."

Then one of the most abusive among the people stood up and said:

"Have you come to us that we should worship God alone and forsake what our forefathers used to worship? Then bring about what you have threatened us with, if you are truthful."

The people were delighted with the man's response. They laughed and mocked Prophet Hud. Then he turned to them and said:

"Already abhorrence and anger from your Lord have befallen you. What, do you dispute with me about names that you and your forefathers invented without authority from God? Then wait; I, too, am among those who wait" (Al Araf 7:65-71). Days passed and as a punishment to the people, God deprived them of rain. For three years, He did not send rain, causing a severe drought in the region. The garden of Iram, which they had boasted of, had dried up. They experienced great difficulties, but still they refused to heed the warning, and continued to wait in vain for rain.

Prophet Hud realized it was a sign of a grave punishment, and decided to warn his people one last time. He went to a place where they gathered and said:

"Will you not avoid disobedience to God in reverence for Him and seek refuge in His protection? Surely I am a trustworthy messenger; I ask for no wage from you, only from the Lord of the worlds. Will you continue to build on very high spots monumental buildings for pleasure and ostentation, and make for yourselves great castles, hoping that you might live forever, and strike and seize in the style of tyrants?"

Prophet Hud objected to the influence that extravagant constructions had on the cultural and spiritual attitude of his nation.

"Follow me, do not disobey He Who has amply provided you with all that you are well aware of — amply provided you with flocks and herds and children, and gardens and springs. Indeed, I fear for you the punishment to come!"

They responded:

> "It is all the same whether you preach, or do not preach. This is the pattern of conduct of our predecessors. And so we are not going to be subjected to any punishment." (Shu'ara 26:123-138)

Prophet Hud grieved. Then the people noticed dark clouds forming in the sky, and they began to rejoice. But their joy was short-lived. The darkness began to generate a sense of fear. The wind rose up suddenly, and a violent storm began. A hurricane of tremendous force overpowered the city. Severe winds battered and destroyed everything. The sturdy buildings, and the powerful people were scattered over the earth like tiny seeds. The city was in ruins.

The only ones to escape with their lives were Prophet Hud and a few believers. Those who had rejected and ridiculed a Messenger of God had been gravely punished.

Reflections

All prophets conveyed the same message, and likewise, their tribulations were similar. Prophets advised people to fear and obey God. They did not say: "I performed my duty, now give me my due," they said: "I came to warn you and protect you," and left their reward to God.

It was a new era in the history of humanity for the people of Ad. Like the Genoese, who constructed castles on the highest mountain peaks, the people of Ad erected walls, towers and castles for protection and recreation. Some claim that the foundation of humanity was nomadic; but humans may have become familiar with civilization because of what their prophets taught them.

The people of Ad wanted to immortalize their civilization, memories and art, and constructed glamorous palaces, monuments and masterpieces. They thought their society would last forever, and their boasting and conceit eventually led them to idolatry. To sculpt and engrave stone with a sense of enduring fame is a sign of an arro-gant culture. If their intention is to glorify themselves rather than God, their constructions were actually built in defiance, monuments of disobedience rather than art. God despises vanity, and punishes the vain.

Believers, like the Prophets, must make every effort to help deprived souls searching for truth. A believer's duty, even toward individuals who have wandered astray, is to guide them to the places where they will learn about God, and to endure any difficulties they may face on the straight path.

WHO IS THE CHILD'S REAL MOTHER?

During the time of Prophet David, a young woman went for a walk with her small child. She found an area of greenery and trees, and sat to rest for awhile. An older lady came and sat beside the young woman. She, too, had a young child; in fact, the children were about the same age.

As the women talked, the children played happily near them. But then the older lady's child crawled into the bushes and disappeared unnoticed. A hungry wolf was hiding in the bushes, and snatched the child's clothing in its teeth, and ran off at great speed. When she heard her child screaming, she ran toward his screams as fast as she could, but it was too late. She ran after the wolf, but it was impossible to catch it.

The younger woman was horrified for her, but the older lady was crafty. She immediately grabbed the younger woman's child from the ground saying, "here is my child." The young woman responded angrily:

"What do you think you are doing? You know very well this child is mine. I realize you are very upset, but I cannot allow you to take my child."

The older lady replied:

"How can this be your child? The wolf ran off with your child, this is mine."

A loud argument erupted between the two women and they were on the verge of fighting when the people nearby suggested they should go to Prophet David. David was known as a man of justice, who would make a righteous decision. The women agreed, and went to Prophet David.

The older lady showed no reluctance to lie, and swore an oath that the child was hers. She called the younger woman a liar, and found witnesses to swear falsely for her to convince Prophet David. Her subterfuge was successful, and David decided that the older woman was the child's real mother.

The younger woman was distraught. In desperation, she suggested:

"If you agree, we can go to Solomon. I will accept whatever he decides."

Solomon was the son of Prophet David, and was known for his wisdom. The older woman was supremely confident in her ability to trick anyone, so she had no objection.

Solomon listened very carefully to each woman. Indeed, the older woman was a convincing and skillful liar. The child's real mother, the younger woman, was unclear and ineloquent, hopeless at expressing herself.

Suddenly Solomon gave an order to one of the guards:

"Fetch me a knife, I will divide the child into two, and give one half of the child to each woman."

On hearing this, the older woman remained calm and said: "I obey your decision sir."

However, when the real mother heard his words, she became frantic. She ran to her child to protect him. With tears rolling down her cheeks, she screamed:

"No, I give in! I do not want anything to happen to my child, I want him to live."

The older woman had shown no sign of fear or compassion for the child, and Solomon realized who the child's mother really was. He handed the child to the young woman.

Reflections

A mother has tremendous compassion for her children, and would face even death without hesitation to save her child from danger. Even in the animal kingdom, a hen will courageously attack a dog to protect her chicks. God granted mothers hearts full of compassion, sensitivity and courage. She worries and suffers grief for her child. If a needle pricks a child's finger, his mother feels the pain as if she was pricked. Even if an adult child of twenty is slightly late returning home, his mother is unable to sleep.

There are ancient fables about a mother's compassion. For example, there once was a young man, deeply in love, who was faced with a brutal demand from his fiancée. The bride-to-be, very jealous of his mother, asked her future husband to bring her his mother's heart. The young man was so besotted that he went and killed his mother. But as he began to remove her heart, the knife slipped and he cut his own finger. He cried: "Mother!" And in response, his mother's heart cried back:, "O, my child! Does it hurt?"

Deceiving people is evil. Even if a person has been deceived, he should never deceive others. Loyalty is one of the greatest virtues. Though in certain situations it may result in loss, we must never stray from the path of truth. God is constantly with those who are truthful.

The trustworthiness of Prophet David and Solomon is clear, because they were honored to judge a dispute involving a cunning, immoral woman. Muslims must portray reliability and trustworthiness to others. As they say, virtue is always admired, even by the enemy.

YOU HAVE LIED

After the people are gathered together on the Day of Judgment, they will be questioned about every word they spoke and every action they performed in this world. On the Last Day, people will have a long or short wait, according to their position in the eyes of God. They will be questioned with no interceder. While a hadith of the Prophet tells us that believers will answer these questions with ease, it also tells us that those who rejected faith will undergo extensive scrutiny.

In addition to the book of deeds, the limbs of the body and the earth will also bear witness to the individual's actions. In the course of the questioning, none will be able to avoid five questions: how they lived their lives, how they spent their youth, how they used their knowledge, where they earned and spent their wealth, and where they used their bodies.

According to a hadith, God will call a man who recited and memorized the Qur'an and ask him:

"Did I not teach you the Qur'an that I revealed to My messenger?"

The man will reply:

"Yes, You taught me, O Lord!"

"What did you do with your knowledge?"

"I recited it day and night and I taught it to others for Your sake, O Lord!"

"You have lied." And the angels, too, will scold the man: "You have lied."

Then God will say:

"You learned and recited the Qur'an so that others would say, 'he recites the Qur'an beautifully, he is a man of great knowledge,' and this is what they said about you." Then the angels will order him to be dragged face down and cast into the Hellfire.

Then a man blessed with various assets and great wealth will be brought forth. God will ask him:

"Did I not provide you with various blessings throughout your life on earth and make you wealthy?"

The man will reply:

"Yes, You blessed me with wealth, O Lord!"

"What did you do with the wealth I granted you?"

"I spent it where You wanted me to, I spent for Your sake and I was never greedy."

"You have lied." And the angels, too, will scold the man: "You have lied."

Then God will say:

"Whatever you gave, you gave so that others would say, 'What a generous man he is,' and this is what they said about you." Then the angels will order him to be dragged face down and cast into the Hellfire.

Then a man who fought in this world and died will be brought forth. God will ask him:

"How were you killed?"

"I was commanded to fight for Your sake. I fought for Your sake until I died as a martyr."

"You have lied." And the angels, too, will scold the man: "You have lied."

Then God will say:

"You fought so that others would say, 'what a courageous man he is,' and this is what they said about you." Then the angels will order the man to be dragged face down and cast into the Hellfire.

Reflections

The true believer is the one who has the most excellent manners. He takes no pride in his worship, never deceives others, and bears no grudges or evil in his heart. Ostentation distances a human from God, and deceit distances a human from both God and society.

When a person performs worship with sincerity while alone, but conceals his worship from others, this is hypocrisy; when a person ignores worship while alone, but performs worship before others, this is a form of polytheism. A believer must constantly examine his relationship with the Creator. If we consider the judgment of others during worship, we are only deceiving ourselves. We must abstain from ostentation and imitating others. There is no value in actions performed to earn the appreciation of others. Wanting others to see and appreciate our good deeds, or wanting others to praise us, is wrong.

Everyone worships according to their ability. Ignoring worship out of laziness is a grave mistake. A believer must fulfill his duties with consciousness of his servitude to God.

THE BOY WHO COULDN'T BE KILLED

O nce upon a time, there lived a king and his magician. As the years passed, the magician gradually grew old and frail. One day, the old magician approached the king and said:

"I am very old. Find me a young boy so that I may teach him my knowledge, and when I die, he can take my place."

The magician began to teach his knowledge to a young boy assigned to him by the king. The boy left home early every morning without fail, and went to the magician to learn new spells.

One day, as he was on his way to the magician, the young boy noticed an old man. He was a learned man who was totally devoted to worshiping God. The young boy began to visit with the elderly man, and eventually began to enjoy his company. Every day he left home, and before he went to the magician, the boy sat with the old man for a while, listening to his words of wisdom.

Once, on his way to the palace, the young boy noticed a crowd gathered by the road. A fierce wild animal was lying in the road, obstructing the path of the passersby. The people were relieved to see the apprentice approaching.

"Look, the magician's apprentice is coming! He can perform magic, and save us from this vicious animal!"

Suddenly, the young boy had an idea. "This is a great opportunity, it will prove to me whether the magician's magic, or the old man's words, are true."

So the young boy performed a horrifying spell. Although the people were afraid of the magic, it had no effect whatsoever on the wild animal. Instantly realizing the truth, the young boy raised his hands up towards the heavens and supplicated. "O Lord! If You are more pleased with the old man's advice than the magician's spells, please kill this animal and allow the people to continue on their journey." Picking up a stone from the ground, he threw it at the animal. It died immediately and the people were free to continue their journey.

Then the young boy told the story to the wise old man.

"My dear son! You are now superior to me. Because of this, you may face certain trials, but whatever happens, never mention me to anybody."

As the days and months passed, the young boy grew in knowledge and faith. With his supplications, he became famous for healing the blind, skin diseases and many other illnesses. He was recognized throughout the land.

One of the king's assistants, who was blind, came to the young boy and pleaded to be cured. The young boy replied:

"I cannot heal anybody, only God has the power to heal. If you believe in God, He will cure you of your blindness."

The young boy raised his hands towards the heavens and prayed to God, and the servant's sight was restored. The cured man returned to the king, and explained what had happened. In astonishment, the king asked who had cured him.

"My Lord cured me!"

"What? Do you mean that I cured you?"

"No, sir! God the Almighty, Who is both your Lord and mine!"

"You claim to have a lord other than me! Who taught you this nonsense? Tell me his name immediately!"

When the king received no reply, he began to torture the servant. Unable to endure the torture, the servant told the king the name of the young boy. The king summoned the boy to the palace, but when he received the same reply, began to torture him too. Unable to resist the harsh punishment, the young boy was eventually forced into telling the king where he could find the old man.

The king called together the three individuals who believed in God, and ordered them to renounce their faith. If they refused, they would face death. When the three did not waver, both the old man and the king's servant were executed. Then the king handed over the young boy to his guards, ordering them to pitch him off a high mountain. Just as he was about to be thrown off the peak, the young boy supplicated:

"O Lord! Save me from the evil of these men!"

Suddenly the ground began to tremble, and the guards themselves were thrown from the mountain. Only one of the king's men survived. He hurried back to the king, and told him what had happened.

Then the king handed the boy over to another group of guards, commanding that if he insisted on his faith, that they should throw him into the deepest part of the ocean. Once again, by virtue of his supplications, the young boy escaped the punishment. Returning to the king, the young boy explained that he would only be successful in killing him if the king did exactly as he said.

Gathering all the people together, the young boy told the king that the only way to kill him was by tying him to a tree, taking an arrow from his pouch and shooting the arrow while saying, "In the name of this child's Lord." The king did exactly as the young boy said. The arrow pierced the young boy's heart, and he died.

The people who witnessed said, "We believe in this child's Lord." The boy had previously called them to faith in the one God, and due to his efforts, many of them already believed.

Upon hearing this, the king became furious and ordered the digging of deep trenches. He had the trenches filled with fire and, one by one, cast the believers into the flames. Among those waiting to be thrown into the fire was a woman carrying a baby who could not yet speak. Like the others, she believed in God. Like the others, her only crime was her belief in God. Brought to the blazing trench, the woman feared being thrown into the flames with her child. Like any mother, she was more concerned for her child's life than her own. Then, by the grace of God, the child said:

"O mother! Be patient, for you are on the right path, the path of truth."

And with the trust and submission granted by virtue of this extraordinary event, the woman threw herself and her child into the rising flames.

Reflections

The young boy possibly symbolized the truth of God, who was protected for a time from the evil of others. Those commanded to kill him instead died by the mercy of God. Their attempts were in vain because God never granted them permission to do so. Perhaps because he had publicly warned the boy, or perhaps because of the boy's own fame and adoring public, the king may have feared certain social complications. Although the reason may not be evident, we can safely make certain assumptions reading between the lines of the story. Though the boy died, the king's reputation was in ruins, and the entire community recognized the existence of the Creator.

Among the story's lessons is that the time on earth given to believers by the Creator should be spent in the most beneficial way possible. Believers should work to improve themselves in this life, making an effort to gain a greater reward in the afterlife. For example, the Almighty declares that one good deed, in certain situations, will be granted the reward of seventy, or even seven hundred good deeds. Therefore, with every seed of prosperity we sow, we may reap up to seven hundred times the reward. And since there is wisdom in every good action, we do not perform them only for the sake of the Hereafter, but also for our life on earth. The signs and practices defined in both the Qur'an, and the Prophet's traditions are an eternal treasure, and therefore must be fully appreciated.

Since the time of the Prophet Adam, peace be upon him, there has been a conflict between truth and falsehood, and without doubt, this war will continue until the Day of Judgment. Although sometimes evildoers appear to be winning, the true victors are, and will always be, the people of faith. If the Almighty wills, He makes babies speak up for His righteous servants. In addition to that of Jesus, there were three instances in which a baby spoke miraculously.

THE BABY WHO RECOGNIZED HIS FATHER

In ancient times, there was a young man named Juraij. Juraij was devoted to his faith, a well-mannered young man who received immense pleasure from worshiping God. Juraij transformed the garden of his home into a place of worship, to perform his prayers in peace. He made a habit of prolonging his worship, as this gave him spiritual satisfaction.

One day he had just begun to pray when his mother called out for him:

"Juraij…Juraij…"

He had the choice of either abandoning his prayers and answering his beloved mother, or continuing to pray and keeping his mother waiting. He thought: "O Lord! I must choose between the prayer and my mother." Halfheartedly, he decided that abandoning worship would be the wrong thing to do, and continued to pray. His mother waited, and when she saw no sign of Juraij, she returned home and went to call him again the following day.

"Juraij…Juraij…"

But again Juraij was seeking refuge in his Creator when she came, and again, he continued to pray.

His mother came again on the third day. Juraij was praying, and once again decided to continue his prayer. His mother was once again forced to return home without seeing her son. She had no idea that he was engaged in worship, and was very angry.

She said: "Son! May God not grant you death until you have experienced the trial of an evil woman!"

Months passed, and Juraij continued his worship as usual. Everyone spoke of Juraij's devotion to God, and how he avoided sin. Nothing could make Juraij abandon his prayers, and everybody knew it.

One day, a woman renowned for her beauty and indecency went to the people and claimed: "I can make Juraij stray from the path of God."

She visited Juraij's place of worship and attempted to allure him while he was praying, but her efforts were in vain. He totally ignored her. No matter what she did, she could not distract Juraij from his prayers.

In her anger, she had an idea. In secret, the woman had an affair with Juraij's shepherd, became pregnant and gave birth to the shepherd's child. To turn the people against him, she claimed that the child belonged to Juraij. The townspeople crowded around Juraij, forcing him to abandon his worship. They began to beat him and even demolished his place of worship. Juraij, unaware of the woman's plot to slander him, called out:

"Why are you beating me? What have I done to you?"

They began shouting at him:

"You dishonorable man! You fornicated with this woman, and she gave birth to your child, but you still have the audacity to portray yourself as being on the path of God."

Because he was strong in his faith, Juraij was patient. He placed all his trust in God, and sincerely believed that his Lord would help him. Then he turned to the people and said:

"Bring me the child."

They brought the child. Juraij stood for prayer, and raised his hands in supplication to his Lord. Lightly touching the baby's stomach, Juraij asked the child:

"Who is your father?"

Suddenly, to the people's astonishment the child replied:

"My father is a shepherd."

The people began to kiss Juraij's hands and beg his forgiveness. They wanted to rebuild Juraij's house of worship in gold to apologize. But Juraij, who loathed ostentation, refused and said:

"Rebuild it from earth, not gold."

Those who had believed the words of a woman of loose morals, rather than those of a man known for his excellent character, felt deeply ashamed. They began to rebuild, in the hope of gaining Juraij's forgiveness.

Reflections

When they are angry, mothers might wrongly curse their children. If something terrible does happen to the child, the mother is the one who will be affected the most. Our parents brought us into this world. It is our duty to respect, show concern, tend to their needs and gain their pleasure. God commands this:

> *Your Lord has decreed that you worship none but Him alone, and treat parents with the best of kindness. Should one of them, or both, attain old age in your lifetime, do not say "Ugh!" to them, nor push them away; and always address them in gracious words. Lower to them the wing of humility out of mercy, and say: "My Lord, have mercy on them even as they cared for me in childhood"* (Al-Isra 17:23–24).

God will never abandon His devoted servant in a time of need. According to a hadith, God will be his eyes to see, his feet to walk, his hand that grasps and tongue to speak. When the servant of God seeks His protection, his Lord will protect him.

NEVER BE DECEIVED BY APPEARANCES

It was a beautiful day, and a woman decided to take her son for a walk to get some fresh air. The woman carried her little boy for quite a distance, and then decided to sit for awhile. She put her son down on the grass to play. After he had played for quite a long time, he began to cry of hunger. Comforting her little boy, the mother picked him up, saying: "Is my little baby hungry? Shall I feed you?" It was his feeding time.

As the woman suckled her baby, she noticed a young man on horseback, galloping in the distance. She envied him, for he was tall and handsome, and appeared to be a powerful man. The mother supplicated: "O Lord! Let my son be exactly like that young man when he grows up."

Suddenly the baby stopped suckling and miraculously began to talk: "O Lord, no! I do not want to be like that man!"

The mother was astonished to hear her little boy speak. In fact, she was so shocked that she did not even realize what he had said. Then the child continued to suckle as if nothing had happened. Suddenly she heard a commotion in the distance. A group of men were beating a servant and shouting at her:

"You evil woman! Not only did you commit adultery, you stole, too. Leave here immediately and never come back."

But the woman denied their accusations, and with tears rolling down her cheeks, pleaded: "No! I am innocent, I am neither an adulteress nor a thief. You are accusing me of something I did not do."

The mother supplicated to God: "O Lord! Please do not allow my son to be like that evil woman when he grows up."

Again, the child stopped suckling, and by the will of God he spoke once more: "O Lord, I want to be like that servant woman when I grow up."

His mother was bewildered to hear her child speak again, and turned to her little boy and asked why he had contradictory supplications to her own. The child replied: "My dear mother, never be deceived by appearances. That man who you envied was actually a cruel person. But the servant woman was innocent, she had not committed any of the crimes they accused her of, and she was a very decent, honorable woman, and this is why I prayed to be like her when I grow up."

Reflections

We can be deceived by what we see. Therefore, whenever we ask for God's favor, we should always pray for what is the best for us.

Satan deceives people by glamorizing evil to appear good, and mocking good to appear evil; his false presentation coincides with the human ego. The human mind and the sum of our experiences is insufficient to comprehend the excellence that results from divine commands, and the evil that results from what is forbidden. Satan encourages humans to overrule their own consciences. Humans are tempted by Satan to do illogical things that will harm themselves or others. Despite their reason, they think they must experience the taste of poison to realize that it kills.

A hadith of the Prophet states: "There are many destitute people who, if they swear by God, He will prove them right." A person's appearance should not deceive a believer. We must judge others by their intentions and their actions, not the accusations of others.

A HUMBLE PROPHET OR A KINGLY PROPHET?

One day, the Prophet sat talking to Gabriel, the angel of revelation, and the Prophet's most loyal Companion. The Prophet told Gabriel that he had not eaten for days. Suddenly, there was a sound like thunder, and an angel descended to the earth.

Gabriel said it was the first time the angel had been sent to earth by God. The angel brought greetings from his Lord and said: "O Messenger of God! Your Lord asks would you rather be a king and prophet or a humble servant and prophet?"

The Prophet turned to look at Gabriel, from whose wisdom he had benefited before. Gabriel said: "O Messenger of God! Be humble toward your Lord!"

God had told His Messenger to be humble in the Qur'an. "Spread your wings over the believers who follow you." (Ash-Shu'ara 26:215) There were other similar verses.

"I choose to be a humble servant and Prophet of God," the Prophet said.

Choosing this, God made the Prophet His shining example of servitude.

Reflections

Though anyone can be servile and led by others, the Prophet chose to be a devoted slave of God from the beginning of his life until the very end. Never did he worship or submit to commands other than those of God. Humility was his defining characteristic, and the Prophet is mentioned frequently in the Qur'an for his servanthood to God. When a Muslim proclaims the testimony of faith, he bears witness that the Prophet is the Messenger of God. Indeed, he is first the servant of God, and then the Messenger of God.

As a sign of this privilege, the Prophet's servitude is announced five times daily throughout the world from every minaret during the call to prayer. In addition to his Prophethood, his servitude is declared to the universe, for his service must necessarily precede his duty as a messenger.

In the Qur'an, God portrays his worship with the words: "Yet, when God's servant rises to pray, they (the jinn) are all but upon him in swarms." (Al-Jinn 72:19)

Arrogance and pride are signs of inadequate perception and a lack of spirituality. A human who has reached spiritual maturity recognizes every blessing as a favor granted by the Almighty Creator, and submits to Him constantly with a sense of gratitude.

Humility earns the admiration of God, and allows a believer to be content despite the reprimands and contempt of others. One who is humble, and lowers his wings has guarded himself from the potential abuse of others, and has chosen the soundest precaution of safety.

"Humility is a sign of one's having become truly human. One sign of humility is that one does not change after obtaining a high position or wealth, learning or fame, or whatever is publicly esteemed. If any of these circumstances causes the person to alter his or her ideas, attitudes, and behavior, he or she cannot be regarded as having attained true humanity or true humility."[14]

---

[14] M. Fethullah Gülen, *Pearls of Wisdom*, Humility, pp.27-28.

WOULD A MOTHER CAST HER CHILD INTO THE FIRE?

Almighty God is merciful to His servants. He caresses us with the warmth of His compassion like heat from the sun. He watches us and never ignores those who turn to Him in supplication.

He is more compassionate to His servants even than a mother is to her child. The Prophet explained God's compassion to his Companions.

After a battle, among the prisoners of war, there was a woman running around frantically, searching for her child. The poor woman hugged every child she saw, and when she realized that it was not her own child, she returned the child to its mother and continued her search again.

The Prophet stood and watched the woman with tears in his eyes. Eventually the woman found her child, and hugged it tightly, unwilling to let go, overcome with love. Pointing to the woman, the Prophet told his Companions:

"Do you see that woman? Do you think she could cast her child into the fire?"

The Companions replied: "No! She could not do it, O Messenger of God!"

Then the Prophet said: "God is more compassionate to His servants than that woman is to her child."

Reflections

Our Lord is the most Merciful of the merciful. When we refer to a man or a woman, we may say "very affectionate" or "very kind." But when we are referring to God we say, "Arhamu'r Rahimin" — the Most Merciful. (Araf 7:151; Yusuf 12:64).

He is more merciful to His servants than a mother is to her child. Indeed, to the extent that we are sincere and loyal toward Him, He will never abandon us. A verse of the Qur'an states, "Your Lord has not forsaken you, nor has He become displeased with you" (Duha 93:3).

God's compassion and mercy are greater than His wrath. It is our duty to approach God's mercy like a gate, a gate that is always open to those who turn to Him.

We must say, "O Lord, You are the most Merciful of the merciful. Never deprive us of Your compassion. Grant us Your Compassion and guide us to the excellence of humanity. Amin."

THE THREE KNOTS OF SATAN

Zahid was a sincere and pious man who enjoyed worshipping God. He had recently begun to wake up during the night to pray before sunrise, which gave him great pleasure and satisfaction. Though it was difficult at the beginning, his body had adapted to waking up at the same time during the night.

Naturally, the one who was troubled most by the worship of this devoted servant was Satan; he never wants a person to be close to God — his duty is to spoil the relationship between God and His servant.

One night, Zahid went to sleep with the intention of waking up for the dawn prayer. As usual, he supplicated to God before falling asleep. But Satan was determined use all his skills, to do whatever was necessary, to prevent Zahid from waking up to pray. Satan decided to delude him by ensuring his sleep was pleasant, and he whispered:

"Sleep, Zahid, sleep. Sleep comfortably, you still have a long night ahead of you. It is still early, you can sleep for awhile longer."

It was almost as if he had tied a knot between Zahid and his prayer. And Satan repeated it three times, like three knots Zahid had to untie before he could pray.

Accompanied by the enticing whispers, Zahid drifted into a deep sleep.

Then suddenly, Zahid bolted awake, and leaped out of bed. If he had slept any longer he would have missed the dawn prayer.

"I must go and pray, time is running out," Zahid thought. Thus the first knot was untied. Then he performed ablution. The second knot was untied. And finally, Zahid stood for prayer, untying the third knot. Zahid was reunited with God.

Meanwhile, Satan was overwhelmed with anger.

"I am never going to give up. I may not have won this time, but I will get my revenge. Even if I am not successful in deceiving Zahid, I will always find others to entice into my traps."

Zahid performed the dawn prayer. Afterward, as the sun rose, he felt contented, refreshed and energetic. He saw the benefits of the prayer throughout the day, which was very productive.

Reflections

Satan is devious. Whatever he does, he does with subtlety, never exposing his real intention. Step by step, he gently entices people who rarely even realize they are being influenced. He whispers, and then smoothly convinces us to take a step. The first step may seem insignificant or trivial, quite far away from anything truly evil. But then other steps follow. Satan convinces humans to take steps, one after another; eventually the individual becomes his servant and slave. Committing trivial sins ultimately leads a person totally astray, into lives of darkness and evil. The pursuit is like a journey you do not realize you are taking. With the initial step, Satan has grasped the reins that lead us toward sin, so we must be alert to avoid it.

The Qur'an states: "O you who believe! Do not follow in the footsteps of Satan. Whoever follows in the footsteps of Satan, (let him know that) Satan insistently calls to all that is indecent and shameful, and all that is evil..." (Nur 24:21).

Satan schemes to ensnare humans with delusion. By luring the heart, he reaches every limb of the body. This is why satanic whispers are first sensed in the heart. Whispers rejected by the heart do no harm, as they did not exceed the boundaries of the imagination. Understanding whether delusions have been rejected by one's heart is easy — if one's heart feels fear or sorrow at the thought of sin, it is a clear sign that the heart rejected Satan's whispers.

Faith strengthens by ignoring satanic delusions; strong reactions are a sign of intense faith. When the Prophet referred to such a reaction he said, "This is true faith!"[15]

---

[15] Muslim, Iman, 211; Musnad 2/456; 6/106.

NADIM'S SIN

In ancient times, there lived a man named Nadim. He was a very quiet and harmless person, who had one bad habit: he drank alcohol. He was aware that it was a sinful act, but he was addicted and found it very difficult to give up drinking.

One day, while he was drinking with his friends, one of them had too much to drink. Nadim was still fairly sober, and watched his friend in astonishment. He was vomiting, swearing and abusing all the people around him. As he attempted to stand up, he stumbled and fell to the ground. Suddenly Nadim thought:

"He is in such a state! I probably behave like this too, and forget my values when I am drunk. I am abusing the body that God entrusted to me. I am never going to drink alcohol again."

Nadim stood up to leave, though all his friends tried to convince him to stay. But Nadim was determined to give up drinking. He returned home, performed the rituals of purification, and turned to the Creator in repentance:

"O Lord, forgive my sins! I will never drink alcohol again, so forgive the sins I have committed, O Lord!"

Then the Lord told His angels:

"My servant has sinned. But he knew that he had a Lord who forgives and punishes sin. I have forgiven his sins."

Several days passed. It was a difficult process for Nadim, because his body was so addicted to alcohol. One day, as he passed by an inn, his friends noticed him and invited him in.

"You all know very well that I repented, and I have no intention of drinking alcohol again. Please do not insist."

They responded by saying:

"Just come in and keep us company for a while. We are not forcing you to drink. Why are you abandoning your best friends just because you have stopped drinking? Where is your loyalty?"

Their words influenced Nadim's judgment. He thought:

"Well, I suppose they are right, there is no harm in sitting with them for awhile, and I will not stay for too long."

The atmosphere inside the inn was tempting. All his friends were drinking. It became impossible for him to resist. Then one of his friends said:

"Hey Nadim, what's the big deal? Have a sip of this, just one sip, there's nothing wrong with that. If drinking is a sin, then God can punish me instead of you."

Before he could think it over, Nadim drank a sip from his friend's glass. And his sip led to an entire bottle.

Afterward, Nadim deeply regretted what he did. He had broken his promise to God, and was ashamed. But he

knew that he had no one else to turn to. So Nadim
returned home, performed the rituals of purification, and
stood before the Lord in utter shame, begging for mercy
and forgiveness:

"O Lord! I repented for my sins, but I went back on
my promise and sinned again. I feel so ashamed of what I
did, but I have no one but You to turn to for forgiveness.
You are the Lord of the universe. Your compassion and
mercy are plentiful. I beg Your forgiveness. O Lord! I
plead with You to forgive Your disobedient servant. Forgive me, and I swear that I will never drink again."

Then God said:

"My servant has sinned again. But he knew that he had
a Lord who forgives or punishes sin. I have forgiven his
sins."

Several days more passed. Unable to resist the temptation, Nadim drank yet again. It was the third time he had
sinned since his atonement. Overwhelmed by regret and
shame, he thought, "How can I possibly ask God to forgive me again?" But this time he was determined. He supplicated to God:

"O Lord, the most Merciful One! I was unable to control myself. Although I repented twice before, I sinned
again. But this is the last time. I give You my word, O
Lord! I will never drink again."

The Creator saw that Nadim was sincere in his remorse
and determination, and said:

"My servant has sinned. But he knew that he had a Lord who forgives or punishes sin. My servant, I have forgiven you."

Reflections

Even if a person sins repeatedly, he must always know where to turn for forgiveness. The Lord is so compassionate that He never turns his devoted servants away. Like the man who killed a hundred people, a person who repents must also abandon the friends with whom and environment in which he sinned. Otherwise, there is a strong chance to fall back into sin.

A person should befriend those who will guide him to the path of truth, friends who, when he looks at them, he remembers God. To restore and strengthen faith, he should gather with such people frequently. Both environment and friends play an important role in faith. People are influenced by their surroundings, and will eventually live like those around him.

THE FRAME-UP

Long ago, there lived a judge renowned for his sense of justice. He heard cases brought before him without considering the wealth or power of either party, and passed judgment according to the truth of claims. He was very popular with the public.

Naturally, the community's elite opposed his decisions. Several wealthy people felt their power justified their actions. Once, a woman named Zanna, was embarrassed before the public due to the judge's ruling, and sentenced to a punishment she deserved. In court, she swore revenge before the judge:

"I will get you back for what you have done! I swear to humiliate you before the entire population."

Several months passed, and Zanna began to put her plan into action. She told her servant to visit the judge, pretending to be her husband. So her servant went to the judge and said:

"Sir, we are having serious problems in our marriage, and we are on the verge of divorce. However, I do not want to divorce my wife. I discussed this with her, and we both agreed that we want your help in solving our disputes. You can decide who is right and who is wrong. Can you come to our house and help us?"

The judge wanted to help save a marriage, and agreed to come. With the servant, he went to the house and entered. The servant guided the judge into Zanna's room, and as soon as the judge entered, the servant closed the door and locked it from the outside.

The judge realized he had been tricked into an evil plot. There was a young child, and several bottles of alcohol in the room. Zanna had ordered her servant to kidnap the child of a woman she despised, and imprisoned the child in her home. Zanna gave the judge three options;

"Listen to me, your honor. You have three choices: be intimate with me, kill this child, or drink this alcohol. If you refuse, I will run outside screaming, and humiliate you before the entire community. Believe me, you will never be able to show your face around here again."

The judge chose what he considered the seemingly lesser evil, and began to drink the alcohol. He drank until he was so intoxicated that he had no idea what he was saying or doing. It had been Zanna's plan all along. She then convinced the drunken judge to kill the young boy, and commit adultery with her. And the servant ran out into the street shouting:

"Help! The judge forced his way into our house, drank alcohol, murdered a child and now he is committing adultery with Zanna!"

Before long, the whole neighborhood had gathered in front of the house. Though nobody could believe it, the judge was guilty. Indeed, being under the influence of alcohol had made the judge do things that would never even have crossed his mind when he was sober.

Reflections

Self-protection is the basis of five principles of religion. The principles, also called necessities, are faith, life, lineage, reason and wealth. In fact, even the world's secular legal systems safeguard these values.

Intoxicating substances cause immense damage to the individual, family, mind, wealth and faith. Avoiding these forbidden substances is, from many aspects, to one's own benefit.

Doctors, psychologists and sociologists agree that alcohol is harmful to the health both physically and spiritually, that it creates serious problems within the family unit, and distances them from society. Eventually drinkers become introverted, unhealthy, problematic individuals, and alcohol causes senility in old age. Alcohol, too, is widely recognized as a main factor in the majority of social problems including divorce, murder and traffic accidents.

In addition, alcohol is an evil that incites other major sins such as gambling and prostitution. An intoxicated person may commit sins that he will regret for the rest of his life, because he is wholly unaware of his actions.

THE ARMY OF BIRDS

It was only a short time before the birth of Prophet Muhammad, peace and blessings be upon him, Abrahah, the governor of Yemen, built a place of worship there to attract the caravans and the travelers visiting the Kabah. He hoped to transform the city of Sana into a major center of trade, but it failed to get the attention expected.

Meanwhile, a few angry Arabs vandalized the building by relieving themselves and soiling the walls. Abrahah was furious, and vowed to destroy the Kabah. He prepared an enormous army, with war elephants leading the expedition. Never before had there been such a strong army.

Abrahah and his army first fought and captured Dhu Nafar. Then they won a battle over the Kuthami tribe, and using the tribe's leader, Nafeal b. Nubayib, forced him to guide them to Mecca. In Taif, the Thaqif tribe cooperated with Abrahah to protect Lat, their deity, and gave Abu Rigal to him as a guide. No earthly force was able to show resistance against the army of war elephants. Witnessing its arrival, the Quraysh believed that the Kabah would be destroyed.

Abrahah's army erected tents at Mugmmas, close to Mecca, and while stealing camels that belonged to Meccans, Abu Rigal died. Among the stolen camels were two hundred camels belonging to Abdulmuttalib, the Prophet's grandfather. Abrahah's envoy, Hinata Al-Himyari, entered Mecca and met with the leaders of Quraysh: They promised not to attack on the condition that they reached the Kabah. He informed said they had come to destroy the Kabah, and that they had no intention of fighting.

Abdulmuttalib went to Abrahah and said:

"Abrahah! I have come to ask for my camels, as they are my family's only source of livelihood. Your men seized my camels, and I want you to return them."

Abrahah replied:

"Since the very first time I saw you, I considered you a man of honor. But now you have come to ask me for your camels instead of asking me to spare the Kabah. I have lost my respect for you. I came here to destroy your Kabah, and the only thing you are concerned with is your camels."

"Abrahah, I own those camels. The Kabah also has an owner. He will protect His house."

Indeed, Abdulmuttalib's words were a warning, but Abrahah lacked understanding. Abdulmuttalib took his camels, and returned to the Quraysh. They left Mecca and went into the nearby mountains to protect themselves from attack.

At dawn, Abrahah proceeded toward Mecca. As they approached the city, the huge elephant leading the expedition suddenly paused, then sat down. They tried to get the elephant back on its feet, but it would not get up. Using sharp objects, they eventually forced the elephant to its feet. But no matter how hard they prodded and pushed, the elephant refused to advance toward the Kabah. It never occurred to any of them that this was their final warning.

A huge flock of birds, similar to swallows, suddenly appeared in the sky. None had seen birds like these before. The birds carried small stones in their beaks and claws, and as they flew over the army, they released the stones. Every soldier hit by one of the stones died instantly. The majority of the army died from the stoning. The others died later, stranded in the desert. One of them was Abrahah, who was wounded in the attack, and died on the journey back to Sana.

God the Almighty had shown to the neighboring tribes, and to the whole of humanity, the fate of those who came to destroy His house.

Reflections

Although this incident, described in Surah al-Fil of the Qur'an, may appear to be connected to a time and place in history, it conveys a warning to humanity. This is a topic in tafsir, commentary on the Qur'an. Through this event, God warns all believers: "Did you not see how I dealt with the people of the elephant? You witnessed this, therefore recognize the value of the favors and blessings I bestowed you."

The birds that bombarded the army with stones was an unprecedented event. This incident may have been the means of preparing for the future prophet. Such miracles often occur just prior to prophethood. The destruction of Abrahah's army occurred in the same year Prophet Muhammad, peace and blessings be upon him, was born.

Besides being a protection of the Kabah, His destruction of the enemy was God's favor to the Quraysh.

THE EARTHQUAKE

Prophet Jethro (Shu'ayb) was sent as a prophet to the people of Median. The people of Median had strayed from faith in the unity of God, and deceived people in trade, particularly in the weight and measures of goods. Using various means of deceit, rich merchants exploited the poor. Prophet Jethro was chosen to warn the Median people, and said:

"O my people! Worship only God: you have no deity other than Him. Manifest proof has assuredly come to you from your Lord. So give full measures, and do not wrong the people by depriving them of what is rightfully theirs, and do not cause disorder and corruption in the land, seeing that it has been so well-ordered. That is for your own good, if you are true believers."

Shu'ayb was calling his people to humanity. But like tribes of the past, they ignored his warnings and tried to stop him from preaching the words of God. They sat on the path leading to his house, and threatened anyone who tried to meet him. But Shu'ayb continued to warn his people, and told them he feared they would face destruction, like the people of Noah, Hud and Salih.

Despite all his efforts, the people of Median rejected truth and justice. They also threatened Prophet Jethro:

"Look Jethro, we swear that if you do not return to our faith, we will drive you out from this land!"

They became deserving of the punishment spoken of by Prophet Jethro. The fate of this nation was like the fate of other tribes who rejected God. Suddenly, a tremendous earthquake shook their city, and everyone fell to the ground, dead.

With the compassion of a prophet, Shu'ayb — who had been forced out from his own country, watched with sorrow the destruction of his people from a distance:

"My poor people! I conveyed to you all the commands of God, I strived for your benefit, and I warned you."

Reflections

When we compare the society of Prophet Jethro and the society of today, we see many similarities. By disassociating religion from social relationships, believers fulfill certain religious commands and neglect others. God and His Messenger declared that greedy or dishonest behavior is antithetical to faith. Muslims must strive to practice the commands of faith in every aspect of life. Religion should not be corralled to the mind alone. We must change injustice with our hands, or if this is not possible, speak out against it. If that, too, is not possible, we must feel badly about it in our hearts, though that is the weakest form of faith.

Prophet Jethro began his mission by declaring the unity of God. He knew that every meaningful law stems from this principle. Without sound faith, it is impossible for people to abandon their mischief. Though the particular deviation of his people was avarice and dishonesty, Prophet Jethro initially called them to worship God alone.

After calling them to the path of God, he then raised the subject of being honest in trade. Naturally it is impossible for people who do not believe in God to manage their own affairs with dignity, never mind establish a society that is just and equitable. The first step of prophethood is to explain the existence and unity of God. Then believers will go on to fulfill their duties of worship, servitude and justice.

WORLDLY POSSESSIONS

One day, Jesus set out on a long journey to invite people to the way of truth and justice. On his way, he met a man. The man said:

"I am travelling in the same direction as you. Do you mind if I keep you company on the journey? It is boring traveling that distance alone."

Jesus agreed, and they began to walk together.

They came to the bank of a stream, and the two travelers were tired and hungry. Jesus had three loaves of bread in his bag, so he ate one and gave one to his travelling companion. He was thirsty, and went down to the stream to drink. When he returned, he noticed that the third loaf of bread was gone. He asked:

"There was another loaf of bread here, did you eat it?"

But the man denied it and said:

"No, I did not eat the bread, and I have no idea who did. I turned around for a moment or two and it disappeared. An animal must have taken it and run off."

Jesus disapproved of the man resorting to lying. Eating the bread was not important, so why did he find it necessary to lie?

After they had rested for a while, the men continued on the journey. A while later, they noticed a deer with her two baby fawns. Jesus called one of the fawns to them. The young deer came over to him, and Jesus slaughtered it. They cooked a portion of the meat and ate it. After they had eaten, Jesus said to the remains of the baby fawn:

"By the will of God, come back to life."

The fawn was resurrected and scampered off. Then Jesus turned to his companion and asked:

"I am asking in the name of God, the One who enabled you to see this miracle, did you eat the loaf of bread?"

The man replied:

"I told you, I have no idea who ate the bread. If I had eaten it I would have told you."

They carried on walking for a while, until they reached a river. Jesus took the man's hand, and they walked across the surface of the water to the opposite side. After they had crossed the river, Jesus asked:

"In the name of He who manifested this miracle before your eyes, did you eat the loaf of bread?"

But the man's reply was the same.

Later they reached a deserted place and sat to rest. Jesus gathered a heap of sand and soil with his hands and said:

"By the will of God, turn into gold!"

And sure enough, the heap of sand turned into gold. Then he divided the gold into three and told the man:

"A third of the gold is mine, a third is yours and the other third is for the man who took the loaf of bread."

Hearing this, the man admitted the truth:

"I ate the third loaf of bread."

Jesus told him:

"Take the gold, it is all yours. I cannot be friends with a man who lies."

And Jesus walked away, leaving the man behind. He was even more delighted, for the gold entirely belonged to him. He placed it carefully into a sack. Just then, two strangers approached him. Eyeing the sack of gold, they pulled out their swords and were about to slay him, when he proposed:

"It is not worth killing a human for worldly pleasures! We can split the gold into three, it is enough for all of us."

The two strangers accepted the seemingly sincere proposal. All three were hungry, so one of the two strangers went to a nearby village to buy food. On his way back, he thought:

"Why should I share the gold with them? If I put poison in their food they will both die, and all the gold will be mine."

At the same time, Jesus' travelling companion and the other man were making a plan:

"Why should we give him a third of the gold? When he returns, we will kill him and the two of us can share the gold ourselves."

As soon as the man returned, they murdered him. Then, laughing about their good fortune, the two men ate the poisoned food. A short time later, the two men died from poisoning. The sack of gold lay unclaimed beside the three dead bodies.

Days later, Jesus was on his journey home and passed by the same spot. When he saw the three bodies and the pile of gold he said:

"This is what happens to those who worship worldly possessions. We should avoid the evil of this world that distances us from God."

Reflections

A believer should never resort to lying, and must distance himself from liars. Truthfulness is the defining characteristic of righteousness. The Prophets lived righteously and encouraged righteousness. In a hadith the Prophet said: "It is obligatory for you to tell the truth, for truth leads to virtue and virtue leads to Paradise, and the man who continues to speak the truth and endeavors to tell the truth is eventually recorded as truthful with God. Beware of telling of a lie, for telling of a lie leads to obscenity and obscenity leads to Hell, and the person who persists in telling lies and endeavors to tell a lie is recorded as a liar with God."

This world is the abode where believers serve and earn Paradise. When life ends, service ends. This world is the abode where believers see the Divine attributes, where we sense God through His characteristics, and endeavor to enter the spiritual world that we sense deep in our souls.

If a believer gives the necessary respect and value to everything, and regulates his actions and behavior in accordance with his Lord, he earns virtue. A believer must balance this world and the Hereafter, and remain steadfast about his values.

The world is the means and opportunity for achievement. Just as we take advantage of opportunities and attempt to become prosperous in this world, so to investments must be made for the Hereafter. One must not forget either world, and we are expected to balance the heart and the mind by doing justice to each. Bediuzzaman Said Nursi said a person should neither rejoice at what he gains, nor grieve at what he loses in this world, and then he will succeed in abandoning this world's acquisitions for those in the Hereafter.

Humans have a strange nature; they behave as if they will live forever in a world to which they are only sent as guests. They struggle with all their might to become rich as quickly as possible. More often than not, humans are impatient, and stray from the path of truth by choosing the quicker, easier means of achieving wealth. A verse of the Qur'an confirms this human weakness: "Human is, by nature, impatient, as if made of haste" (Al-Anbiya 21:37). The Prophet also described this characteristic of humans: "If the son of Adam owned two valleys full of gold, he is sure to want a third. Only soil (of the grave) can satisfy his avarice."

Naturally, this does not mean that humans should not work for this world. But hasty get-rich-quick schemes, rather than real effort and sacrifice, lead to ruin in both worlds. And whatever effort and sacrifice we make for the sake of this world alone, must be made to an even greater degree for eternal life.

THE BEST NEWS FOR SATAN

Satan and his accomplices have just one aim: to cause humans to stray from the true path by enticing them to do what God dislikes. Satan loathes humans, because mankind caused him to be expelled from the divine presence. When he defied the command to prostrate before Adam, he severed his connection with God, and Satan lost his place among the angels and was abandoned. Then he began to seek revenge. Satan asked God to be given reprieve until the Day of Judgment. It was granted. Rather than repenting for his sin and seeking God's forgiveness, Satan became even more rebellious, and chose a target that would keep him occupied until the Last Day. His target was humankind.

Overwhelmed with vengeance, Satan and his accomplices schemed to deceive humans. Satan taught his accomplices various deception tactics. Afterward, they reported their accomplishments.

One accomplice said:

"I put temptation in a human's soul to drink alcohol, and I was successful. This is how I led him astray."

Satan was not especially pleased, and shook his head.

Then the next accomplice spoke:

"I lured a man to gamble. He lost everything except his house. So I tempted him by saying, 'Risk your home, too, if you win you will retrieve everything you lost.' He gambled and lost his home as well, and now the man and his children have nowhere to live."

Satan was not overwhelmed with this news, either. He was waiting for something more thrilling.

Then it was the next accomplice's turn:

"I did some mischief-making between a man and his wife, and I made them argue. Their marriage was an example to everyone around them, but now because of me they have separated. They abused each other to an extent that reconciliation became impossible. The couple is on the verge of divorce."

Satan smiled with joy. He summoned all of his accomplices and said:

"This is the news I was waiting for. You accomplished the greatest of all duties, and I congratulate you on your achievement. You have pleased me immensely."

Satan summoned his favored accomplice, patted him on the back and sat the accomplice at his right hand. In doing so, he insinuated: "One of the acts I love the most is separating a married couple, and the one who achieves this deserves his place beside me."

Reflections

A believer must supplicate constantly for God's protection against the evil of Satan. Even if we seek refuge in God from the whispers of Satan a thousand times daily, it is still insufficient. Satan is so devious, and has so many tricks and ploys of manipulation, that it is impossible for any human to contend with him. But Satan only sows the seeds of temptation in the hearts of humans and guides them to evil, he does not create the actual result. He Who is the Creator of good and evil, and of light and darkness, is God. We should be prepared for the delusions and traps of Satan, and must take refuge in God. When God grants His mercy and blessings, Satan is prevented from achieving his goals.

One of scenes that Satan loves the most is the separation of married couples. Of all things that are allowed in Islam, divorce is the one God hates the most. A couple decided to be a family, and vowed to share joy and sorrow, support each other through times of wealth and poverty, and spend this life and the afterlife together. During a quarrel, a couple must avoid abusive language. Satan entices couple to abuse one another, which leads to discord and ultimately divorce.

People say to never say or do anything you may regret later. Spouses must face each other at one time or another, if not in this world, then in the Hereafter. Words of abuse such as: "you are not you so special," or "I should never have married you," will cause irreparable damage in the marriage.

Whatever the circumstances, we must control our tempers. We must think before we talk and remember that we will have to account for every single word we said. One punishment of talking before thinking is the deep regret of our words later. There are many divorced people in the world today who are pained by the words they spoke in anger.

REFERENCES

Abdulbaki, M. Fuad, *Mu'cemu'l Müfehres li Elfazi'l Kur'ani'l Kerim*, Istanbul: 1987.

Abu al-Baqa, *Al Kulliyyah*, Beirut: 1993.

Abu Dawud, *As-Sunan*, I-II, Muassasatu'l Kutub as-Sakafiyyah Beirut: 1988.

Arpaçukuru, Osman, *Peygamberimizin Anlattığı Hikayeler* (Stories Conveyed by the Prophet), Elest Publishers, Istanbul 2005.

Bayhaqi, *Sunan al-Kubra*, Hyderabad.

Bukhari, *Sahih al-Bukhari*, I-VIII, Daru'l-Fiqr, Beirut: 1994.

Davudoğlu, Ahmet, *Sahih-i Müslim Tercemesi ve Şerhi*, (An Interpretation and Commentary of Sahih al-Muslim), Sönmez Neşriyat, Istanbul: 1973.

Dölek, Adem, *Edebi Açıdan Hadislerde Teşbih ve Temsiller*, Erzurum Cultural and Education Foundation (EKEV) Publications, Erzurum: 2001.

Eren, Şadi, *Kur'an'da Teşbih ve Temsil*, Işık Yayınları, Istanbul: 2002.

Gülen, M. Fethullah, *Sonsuz Nur*, I-III, Nil Publications, Izmir: 1997

__, *Prizma* 1-3, Nil Publications, Izmir.

__, *Ölçü veya Yoldaki Işıklar*, Nil Publications, Izmir 2005.

Hakim, *Al-Mustadrak*, Beirut: 1990.

Haythami, *Majma uz-Zawaid*, Beirut.

Ibn Hibban, *Sahih Ibn Hibban*, Beirut: 1984.

Ibn Hammam, Abdurrazzak, *Al-Musannaf*, Beirut: 1983.

Ibn Hanbal, Ahmad, *Al-Musnad*, I-VI, Istanbul: 1982.

Ibn Huzayma, Sahih Ibn Huzayma, Beirut: 1975.

Ibn Kathir, *Tafsir al-Qur'an al-Azim*, Cairo.

Ibn Majah, *Sunan Ibn Majah*, I-II, Beirut.

İbrahim Canan, *Kütüb-ü Sitte Muhtasarı Tercüme ve Şerhi*, Ankara 1988.

Jurjani, *At-Tarifat*, Beirut: 1996.

Malik ibn Anas, *Al-Muwatta*, Istanbul: 1992.

Muslim, *Sahih al-Muslim*, I-V, Beirut.

Nasai, *Sunan An-Nasai*, I-VIII, Daru'l-Marifah, Beirut: 1992.

The Qur'an (with Annotated Interpretation in Modern English), translated by Ali

Ünal, The Light Inc., New Jersey: 2007.

Qutb, Sayyid, *Fi Zilal al-Qur'an*, Beirut: 1985.

Ramahurmuzi, *Kitab al-Amsal al-Hadith*, Istanbul.

Tirmidhi, *Al-Jami as-Sahih*, Beirut.